A Practical Guide to the Advanced Placement

English Literature and Composition
Examination

by

Duane Earnest

English Instructor
Detroit Lakes Community
Senior High School

D0925239

Plan Press, Inc.
"Teachers Writing for Students"
921 Pembina Trail
Detroit Lakes, Minnesota 56501

Acknowledgments

To my wife, Julia Lucca Earnest, and to my three daughters: Crystal Earnest, who is soon to be an English teacher herself, Bridgette Earnest, who is now a freshman in college, and Erin Earnest, who will have me as a teacher next year. Thanks for your support even though my time spent writing has been at the expense of your time with me.

Author: Duane Earnest

Publisher: Plan Press, Inc.

Managing Editor: Vern Schnathorst
Developmental Editor: Rob Ullyott

Cover Art: K. C. Skinner
Text Cover: Nicholas Bieter &
            Crystal Earnest

Printer: Midwest Printing
         Detroit Lakes, MN 56501

ISBN 0 - 9655850 - 1 - 8

For information write: Plan Press, Inc.
                       "Teachers Writing for Students"
                       921 Pembina Trail
                       Detroit Lakes, MN 56501

First Edition

AP and Advanced Placement are trademarks of the College Board, which has not participated in the development of or endorsed this publication. Publications from the AP College Board have been the major source of reference for writing this book. Authors from the AP Suggested Reading list have been categorized by time period, checklists for grading essays have been compiled by examining the rubrics used to grade previous essays, inferences have been made about the types of essay and multiple-choice questions by examining the previous tests given, and Practice tests have been compiled using previous AP tests as models. All these AP publications can be obtained by writing to: The Advanced Placement Program, P.O. Box 6670, Princeton, New Jersey 08541-6670.

Permission has been given to reprint the following excerpts:

K.C. Skinner. All art work has been created by K.C. Skinner, a student at Detroit Lakes, and used in this book with his permission.

Nicholas Bieter and Crystal Earnest. The text for the back cover has been created by Nicholas Bieter and Crystal Earnest and use with their permission.

Dylan Thomas, "Do Not Go Gentle into that Good Night" from THE POEMS OF DYLAN THOMAS. Copyright © 1952 by Dylan Thomas. Reprinted by premission of New Directions Publishing Corp.

A careful effort has been made to secure permission to reprint copyright materials and to make acknowledgement of their use. Any error of omission is purely inadvertent and will be corrected in subsequent editions if written notice is sent to Permissions Department, Plan Press, Inc., 921 Pembina Trail, Detroit Lakes, MN 56501.

Student Acknowledgments

Thanks to the following students for their invaluable help in finding passages, writing questions, grading papers, and field-testing all exams:

Karla Ash, Sarah Augustin, Sarah Baker, Heidi Bauer, Jennifer Birzneiks, Kara Birznieks, Nick Bowers, Jaime Bruflodt, Devon Brenk, Jade Buermann, Luke Burroughs, Amy Cornelius, Lori Dahring, Randy Fairbanks, Jenny Flottemesch, Emily Fishback, Amy Friendshuh, Andrea Grabow, Jolynn Garnes, Charlie Haggart, Katie Hagle, Nerissa Haisley, Reid Heckman, Kent Heimark, Eric Heyer, Kent Hoeglund, Derek Hopper, Kristen Husby, Phillip Imholte, Nathan Ittner, Jenni Jacobs, Shane Jahnke, Erica Johnson, Kristina Johnson, Joni Johnston, Erin Jorgenson, Becky Koshnik, Ryan Kotta, Alissa Kovala, Dan Lee, Chris Lahren, Birk Larsen, Amy Lehrke, Liz Linquist, Greg Luhman, Jill Mack, Jodi Mallow, Ben Matter, Jay Matter, Angie McKenzie, Cassie Meyer, Mike Miller, Josie Musquiz, Becky Newton, Matt Nustad, Angie Nyland, Amy Olson, Billi Jo Olson, Lisa Olson, Leslie Parker, Stacey Pavelko, Erin Pentinnen, Steph Rasmussen, Ruth Rhoades, Erin Rogers, Karly Russness, Anita Salmela, Naomi Salmela, Kelly Schlauderaff, Steph Schmitz, Adam Schneider, Kris Seabloom, Erin Seaworth, Katy Skogmo, Mary Solie, Tina Sonnenberg, Jill Steinmetz, Tracy Stoltenburg, Anne Stowman, Nate Swanberg, Terri Sundbom, Gabe Sunram, Tina Taves, Matt Taylor, Marit Thorsgard, Michelle Tucker, Robert Wagner, Luke Weekley, Jill White, Wade Whitworth, Laurie Wolfe, Jill Wothe, and Renee Zeeman.

Table of Contents

Preface

The following *Practical Guide to the Advanced Placement English Literature and Composition Examination* is designed to be used as a complement to the already existing excellent literature classes throughout the United States. It is to be used as a resource, as a guide to enrich your present curriculum, making it more AP specific. Using this text in this way, the student will learn to read more perceptively and write more maturely -- an honorable goal for any English instruction.

I wrote this book in conjunction with the writing of *A Practical Guide to the Advanced Placement English Language and Composition Examination*. The Language Revision chapter in the AP Language Guide has been replaced by separate chapters here in Poetry, Prose, and Drama. Other differences between the two examinations are specifically addressed in each of the appropriate chapters.

All inferences made are based on my examinations of various AP Literature publications and tests given from 1970 to 1996. I designed AP essay questions on materials I was teaching, developed checklists for grading essays by examining rubrics used to grade previous essays, and wrote full-length multiple-choice tests using previously published AP Literature tests as models. With each task, I was able to make predictions about AP Literature expectations. This book is a result of those studies.

Chapter One: Suggested Reading

The Advanced Placement Program provides a list of suggested authors in *A Student Guide to the AP English Courses and Examinations*. Chapter One of this book places these authors in the appropriate time periods. Since Advanced Placement selects writers for their examinations based on a range of diversities, the AP student should do the same. Read some from each time period; read a good selection of female and multi-cultural authors; read a good variety of genres, etc.

Chapter Two: The Essay

The Essay section offers a detailed analysis of the types of questions asked since 1970, strategy suggestions for writing various types of style analyses and open essays, and checklists and rubrics for each type of question asked.

Students Grading Students

Four years ago I decided that I would have my students grade each others' papers in a reader's response fashion. I spent much time in the beginning teaching them to be positive in their remarks. Once this message was understood, the students had difficulty being critical enough. Without objective direction, I began to realize my experiment with student grading was failing. My students were feeling great about themselves, but their writing was getting worse!

Turning to the rubrics created by the College Board to grade previous AP essays, I discovered that each set of descriptions had nine distinct elements. By putting these in the form of checklists, I now had a vehicle for my students to use in effectively grading other papers on the nine point scale used by AP.

Each essay written is now graded by three people -- two students and myself. I grade them holistically, putting a mark of 1 - 9 in my grade book. Once they receive a paper to grade, students refer to the checklists on pp. 38-51. Using these as a guide, they fill out a generic cover sheet (see pp. 38-39 in Chapter Two or see the separate Teacher's Guide Addendum) naming the type of essay, checking appropriate items and making reader's responses, ultimately arriving at a mark of 1 - 9. Using the checklists has been the key to effective student grading. Using the checklists as a guide, the reader responses are still friendly, but they are now also more critically appropriate than the "Nice job, Joe!" responses I was getting earlier.

This checklists system also encourages much beneficial dialogue. If the graders' marks vary more than two points from mine, I check with the graders. Once the students get their own papers back, they are allowed to negotiate the score with me whenever they can defend parts of their paper that deserve a better grade. I now spend less time reading papers and more time talking about papers. My students now benefit with improved writing skills.

Chapter Three: Multiple-Choice

The Multiple Choice section offers strategy suggestions for taking tests, and a detailed analysis of the types of questions AP asks. The information in this chapter allows students and teachers to collaboratively write multiple choice questions for any materials taught.

Chapter Four - Poetry
Chapter Five - Prose
Chapter Six - Drama

These chapters are devoted to helping students become better readers by providing them with the right types of questions to ask. These types of questions appear in many textbooks. The questions in these chapters, however, are arranged in a three-step approach to aid the student in brainstorming and eventually writing the type of close reading essays required of the Advanced Placement Literature examination. This three step approach is as follows:

    1. What is the meaning?

    2. How do the language devices create meaning?

    3. So what?

Chapter Seven: Creative Suggestions

Contests, games, and other creations !

Chapter Eight: Writing Prompts

Various types of formal, informal, long term, and impromptu writing .

Chapter Nine: Glossary

Advanced Placement terms defined.

Chapter Ten: Practice Tests

Sample essays, rubrics, and multiple- choice tests that are included have been compiled by my students through my guidance. These tests were field-tested by my students. After taking the tests, we changed the wording of those questions which most people got wrong. The multiple choice section tests vocabulary, point of view, pronoun reference, meaning, rhetoric, diction, sentence structure, effect, tone, and organization. I use these tests at various times throughout the year to measure my students' learning. They can either be given in one three hour sitting, or separately within the time constraints of the regular classroom.

Test Results

Each sample test ends with the checklists, rubrics, and results of essay writing. I chose to exclude answers and explanations for the three full multiple-choice tests because I wanted these to be used as graded tests in my classroom. These answers and explanations are available in a separate teacher's key addendum.

This book is designed to be a companion textbook to the excellent curriculums already taught in AP classrooms around the country. In the hands of each student, this book can ensure more success in the AP classroom, giving students the potential to succeed on the eventual AP English Literature exam, and ultimately, helping students to become better prepared for college courses.

Chapter One: Suggested Reading-Literature and Composition AP

*Read
Actively-
Take Notes!*

SUGGESTED READING
Literature and Composition -- AP

	Middle Ages (1300-1400)	Renaissance (1485 - 1660)	Restoration (1660 - 1800)
Poetry	Geoffrey Chaucer.	**John Donne,** George Herbert, Ben Johnson, Andrew Marvel, John Milton, **William Shakespeare.**	Anne Bradstreet, Alexander Pope.
Drama	Sophocles (406 BC?)	Ben Johnson, **William Shakespeare.**	Wm Congreve, Oliver Goldsmith, Moliere.
Novel, Short Story			Henry Fielding, Jonathan Swift.
Expository Lit			**Joseph Addison,** James Boswell, Samuel Johnson, Richard Steele.

NOTE: This Suggested Reading List is published in the *Student Guide to the AP English Courses and Examinations,* 1996, 1997. However, this list does not place the authors in the time periods.

SUGGESTED READING
Literature and Composition -- AP

	Romantic (1800 - 1901)	Victorian (1832-1901)
Poetry	William Blake, Lord Byron, Samuel Taylor Coleridge, **John Keats,** Edgar Allan Poe, **Percy Bysshe Shelly,** William Wordsworth.	**Matthew Arnold,** Robert Browning, **Emily Dickinson,** Gerard Manley Hopkins, Alfred Lord Tennyson, Walt Whitman.
Drama	Anton Chekhov.	**Henrik Ibsen,** Oscar Wilde.
Novel, Short Story	Jane Austen, Emily and Charlotte Bronte.	**Kate Chopin, Stephen Crane,** Charles Dickens, **Frederick Douglass,** George Eliot, Thomas Hardy, **Nathaniel Hawthorne,** Herman Melville, Leo Tolstoy, **Mark Twain,** Edith Wharton.
Expository Lit	Thomas Carlyle, Ralph Waldo Emerson, William Hazlitt, Charles Lamb, Henry David Thoreau.	Matthew Arnold.

NOTE: This Suggested Reading List is published in the *Student Guide to the AP English Courses and Examinations,* 1996, 1997. However, this list does not place the authors in the time periods.

SUGGESTED READING
Literature and Composition --
Modern (Twentieth Century)

Poetry	W. H. Auden, Elizabeth Bishop, E. K. Braithwaite, Gwendolyn Brooks, Lorna D. Cerventes, H. D., Rita Dove, T. S. Eliot, Robert Frost, Joy Harjo, Seamus Heaney, Garrett Hongo, Langston Hughes, Philip Larkin, Robert Lowell, Marianne Moore, Sylvia Plath, Adrienne Rich, Leslie Marmon Silko, Cathy Song, **Dylan Thomas**, Derek Walcot, Richard Wilbur, William Carlos Williams, William Butler Yeats
Drama	Edward Albee, Amira Baraka, Samuel Beckett, Lorraine Hainsberry, Lillian Hellman, David Henry Hwang, Arthur Miller, Sean O'Casey, Eugene O'Neill, Harold Pinter, Luigi Pirandello, George Bernard Shaw, Sam Shepard, Richard Brinsley Sheridan, Tom Stoppard, Luis Valdez, Tennessee Williams, August Wilson.
Novel, Short Story	Chinua Achebe, Rudolfo Anaya, Margaret Atwood, James Baldwin, Saul Bellow, Raymond Carver, Willa Cather, Sandra Cisneros, John Cheever, Colette, Joseph Conrad, Anita Desai, Ralph Ellison, Louise Erdich, William Faulkner, F. Scot Fitzgerald, Ford Madox Ford, E. M. Forster, Ernest Hemingway, Zora Neale Hurston, Kazuo Ishiguro, James Joyce, Maxine Hong Kingston, Joy Kogawa, Margaret Laurence, D. H. Lawrence, Bernard Malamud, Katherine Mansfield, Gabriel Garcia Marquez, Bobby Ann Mason, Carson McCullers, Toni Morrison, Bharati Mukherjee, Vladimir Nabokov, Flannery O'Conner, Cynthia Ozick, Katherine Anne Porter, Jean Rhys, John Updike, Luisa Valensuela, Alice Walker, Evelyn Waugh, Eudora Welty, John Edgar Wiedman, Virginia Woolf, Richard Wright.
Expository Lit	Gloria Anzaldua, Jesus Colon, Norman Mailer, Mary McCarthy, John Stuart Mill, George Orwell, Lewis Thomas, Barbara Tuchman, Virginia Woolf.

Chapter Two: The Essay Section- Literature and Composition AP

*"ESTABLISH
A
POSITIVE
ATTITUDE!"*

The Essay - Literature & Composition

Suggestions for Writing Any Essay

1. The essay should be long enough to answer the question. An incomplete essay will get a low score; however, if you have written all you can write, go on to the next question. Think in terms of 300 to 500 words (two or three pages). Quality is better than quantity. Good essays have the following three things in common. They:

A. Answer all parts of the question fully;

B. Support with unified, specific, adequate, accurate and representative evidence; and

C. Write maturely.

2. Make your handwriting as neat as possible. Use a ball point pen. An erasable pen will allow you to make revisions more neatly. Write on one side of the paper. Write slowly enough to maintain a high level of neatness.

Write Naturally

1. Read the question, making sure you understand the requirements. You are always asked to make an interpretation about how the author manipulates the language to create meaning. Since all passages are selected because of their complexity of meaning, think in terms of organizing around that complexity.

2. Read the passage actively. Brainstorm by circling evidence (rhetorical or stylistic devices listed in the question) that could be used to show how the author develops the content (attitude, effect, characterization, plot, theme . . .) of the essay.

3. Write a strong opening sentence. Don't write flowery, general beginnings. Get right to the point. Rather than force the same 5 paragraph model into every passage, simply write naturally about how the author creates meaning through manipulation of language.

The Essay – Literature and Composition

Typical Questions

The three forty minute essays on the Literature and Composition Exam usually follow a consistent pattern: one question on a passage of prose, one question on a poem, and one question on a work chosen by the student (usually called the "open" question). One variation may occur. Instead of writing on one passage or poem, the student may be asked to contrast two passages or two poems.

Prose Passage

The following is a generic composite of some of the prose questions asked since 1970. These prose questions can be divided into 3 different types of questions: Tone-Attitude-Point of View, Effect, Literary Elements, or Comparison or Contrast.

Applying these questions to any prose reading assigned can improve your critical reading ability and increase your chance to score higher on the AP exam.

Tone, Attitude, Point of View: Show, explain or demonstrate how . . .

1. The speaker establishes his/her attitude toward the coming of a season.

2. The author's style reveals his/her feelings about the family he/she describes.

3. The writer establishes an attitude toward a family member's death. Using specific references to the text, show how the author's manipulation of language serve to convey his/her attitude.

4. The writer has an attitude toward ____ and therefore makes certain assumptions about human nature. Define precisely what that attitude and those assumptions are and analyze how the writer uses the language to convince the reader of the rightness of his/her position.

5. The author directs the reader's perceptions of the characters in the opening of a novel through his use of such stylistic devices as ___, ____, ____, and ___.

6. The author uses stylistic devices to convey his/her views on a conception of leisure which has lost its place in the society of his/her own time.

7. The author's use of techniques define ____'s character. Be sure to describe the author's attitude toward the ____.

8. The style and tone of the passage helps to express the author's attitudes.

9. Narrative techniques and other resources of language are used by the author to characterize ____ and ____'s attitude toward____.

10. The author conveys his view of ____ through the use of such elements as ____, ____, ____, and ____.

The following language devices are named as suggestions for the writer to consider when analyzing how the author creates attitude: diction - syntax - tone - choice, selection, and presentation of detail - imagery - narrative structure - syntax.

Effect: Show, explain or demonstrate how . . .

1. The world and the way of life described in the passage creates an overall effect.

2. The writer uses ____, ____, and ____ to produce an effect on the reader.

3. The blend of ___, ___, and ____ creates an effect.

The following language devices are named as suggestions for the writer to consider when analyzing how the author creates effect: diction - syntax - imagery - tone - humor - pathos and the grotesque.

Literary Elements: Characterization, plot, setting, etc.)
Show, explain or demonstrate how

1. Two people are "naturally suited" for one another.
2. The author prepares the reader for the character's unwillingness or inability to act. Consider at least two elements of
fiction such as ____, ____, ____, ____.
3. The order of events have significance.
4. The author's presentation of details is intended to shape the
reader's attitudes toward the setting he describes. Give specific attention to the function of ____, ____, ____, ____.
5. This passage provides a characterization and evaluation of
____ more than of ____.
6. The author dramatizes ____'s adventure. Consider such
elements as
7. The author uses literary techniques to characterize the main
character .

The following literary techniques are named as suggestions for the writer to consider when analyzing how the author reveals a literary element of the story: theme - symbol -
setting - image - characterization - word choice - imagery -
phrasing - sentence structure - diction - imagery - narrative
pace - and point of view.

Comparison/Contrast: Show, explain or demonstrate how

1. The nature of each speaker, his assumptions about his audience, and the effects he wants to have on ____ differ in each
passage. Consider the ___ and ___ of each passage.
2. Each author's ___ and ___ is intended to shape the reader's
attitudes toward ____.
3. Two eye-witness accounts of ____s show different attitudes.
Consider the different effects on the reader of the two accounts.
4. The writer makes revisions from the earlier to the later draft
that change the effect of how the experience of ____ affected
his attitude toward language. Discuss the probable reasons
for the writers additions and deletions and the ways in which
those revisions change the effect of the paragraph.

5. A writer differentiates between the writing of two other authors. Analyze his attitude toward each writer and the devices he uses to convey those views.

The following devices are named as suggestions for the writer to consider when analyzing how the authors create different attitudes, effects, personalities, and/or assumptions: diction - sentence structure - presentation of details.

Poetry Passage

The following is a generic composite of the types of poetry questions asked since 1970. These poetry questions can be divided into 4 different types of questions: Tone-Attitude-Point of View, Meaning, or Comparison or Contrast.

Applying these questions to any poetry reading assigned can improve your critical reading ability and increase your chance to score higher on the AP exam.

Tone, Attitude, Point of View: Show, explain or demonstrate how . . .

1. The speaker's attitude toward a person is described in a poem.
2. The _____ of the last stanza of the poem is related to the speaker's earlier view of himself and his view of how others see him.
3. The poet's _____ reveals his attitude toward the two ways of _____ mentioned in the poem.
4. The speaker's attitude toward _____ in the last sestet is related to her attitude toward _____ in the first octave. Using specific references from the text, show how _____ and _____ contributes to the reader's understanding of these attitudes.
5. The language of the poem reflects the changing perceptions and emotions of the speaker toward _____. Develop your essay with specific references to the text of the poem.
6. The attitude of _____ and _____ are contrasted. Through careful analysis of _____ and _____, show how this contrast is important to the meaning of the poem.

7. The language of the poem reflects both the neighbor's and the narrator's perception ____. Discuss how the portrayal of ____ is enhanced by such features as ____, ____ and ____.

8. The ____, ____ and ____ of the soliloquy from ____ conveys the King's state of mind.

9. The poet's use of language reveals the speaker's attitude toward the woman's death.

10. The poem's ____, ____ and ____ trace the speaker's changing responses to encountering unfamiliar aspects of the natural world.

11. The speaker uses the various ____ of the poem to reveal his attitude toward the nature of ____.

The following stylistic devices are named as suggestions for the writer to consider when analyzing how the poet creates attitude: imagery - diction - verse form - language - devices of sound - allusions - syntax - tone.

Meaning: Show, explain or demonstrate how . . .

1. The conceptions of ____ in lines 1-34 differ than those in lines 35-60.

2. The ____ and ____ reveal both its literal and figurative meanings. In your discussion, show how both these meanings relate to the title.

3. The poem's ____, ____, and ____ prepare the reader for the final response.

4. ____, ____, ____ convey meaning in the poem .

The following stylistic devices are named as suggestions for the writer to consider when analzing how the poet creates meaning: organization of the poem - use of concrete details - diction - figurative language - language - imagery - structure - point of view.

Comparison/Contrast: Show, explain or demonstrate how

1. The characteristics of the second poem make it better than the first poem. Refer specifically to the details of both poems.

2. The attitudes toward the coming of a season implied in these two poems differ from each other. Refer specifically to the texts.

3. The two poems presenting encounters with_____ have different attitudes (toward nature, toward the solitary individual, etc.). Distinguish between the attitudes expressed in the poems and discuss the techniques that the poets use to present the attitudes.

4. The _____, _____, and _____ of the verse in the two major sections of the same poem are different in tone and content.

5. The following two poems have similarities and differences. Consider _____ and _____ when analyzing these differences.

6. The _____, _____, _____, and _____ contrast the speakers' different views of _____ in the two poems.

The following stylistic devices are named as suggestions for the writer to consider when contrasting two passages: diction - imagery - movement - theme - style - speaker - diction - form - tone.

The Essay -
Literature and
Composition
Types of Prose/ Poetry Questions

TONE: This question appeared 21 times in the last 25 years. The task of this essay is to analyze how the author/poet uses the language (presents the events in the story, or manipulates point of view) to establish the author's (character's, poet's, or speaker's) attitude (or feelings) toward someone or something. The question will ask you to address 3 to 6 stylistic and rhetorical devices (such as diction, syntax, selection and presentation of details, imagery, narrative structure, verse form, devices of sound, allusions, and other resources of language) which are used by the author to convey that view.

LITERARY ELEMENTS: This question appeared seven times in the last 25 years. Below is a composite wording of these exams. The task of the question is to describe the significance of a basic element of the work (plot, conflict, characterization, or setting) or define the attitude that the author would like the reader to adopt toward an element of the work; and analyze its stylistic, narrative and persuasive devices, or analyze how the author uses the resources of language (such as theme, symbol, setting, image characterization, word choice - diction, imagery, phrasing, sentence structure, narrative pace, point of view, concrete language and structure) to achieve his/her purpose, or analyze the rhetorical strategies the author employs to promote that attitude.

EFFECT: This type of question appeared four times since 1970 in the form of comparison/contrast questions, poetry passage analyses, or prose passage analyses. Following is a composite wording of these questions: The effect of world and the way of life described or the effect of the revisions made from an earlier draft, or the differing effects the writers want to have on the audience, is created by the writer's use of diction, syntax, imagery, tone, humor, pathos, and the grotesque.

COMPARISON - CONTRAST questions are far more prevalent on the AP Literature Examination than on the AP Language Examination. This type of question appeared 11 times since 1970 in the form of prose or poetry passages. Following is a composite of these types of questions: How do such language devices as diction, sentence structure, presentation of details, revisions, imagery, movement of verse, form and tone present different attitudes, different views of the nature of each speaker or writer, different assumptions, or different effects?

MEANING   This question appeared 4 times on the poetry exam. The task of the question is to define how conceptions differ from one stanza to another, or to reveal literal and figurative meanings, or to prepare the reader for the final response. In your discussion, show how these meanings relate to the title, or are created by such things as organization of the poem, use of concrete details, diction, figurative language, imagery, language, structure, or point of view.

Check List for any Style Analysis

1. Identify the author's or speaker's attitude, tone, point of view; OR identify the work's most significant literary element, meaning, or effect.
2. Use most of the body of the essay to analyze aptly and specifically how the author or poet uses selected resources of language, or makes literary or poetical choices to reinforce that view, accomplish that meaning, or achieve that effect.
3. Make sure to show the relationship between each particular language feature and the creation of the author's or speaker's attitude, tone, point of view; OR the work's most significant literary element, meaning, or effect. Do not simply paraphrase the passage or discuss in general the use of particular literary or stylistic devices or catalogue various literary or stylistic elements in the passage without relating them to the author's intended or probable attitude, tone, point of view; OR the work's most significant literary element, meaning, or effect.
4. Answer the entire question; address each rhetorical device listed in the question.

5. Use an adequate amount of evidence (a minimum of three quotes per paragraph) to show how each stylistic or literary device conveys the author's intended or probable attitude, tone, point of view; OR the work's most significant literary element, meaning, or effect.

6. Demonstrate an ability to control a wide range of the elements of effective writing by using correct, specific, and mature diction, proper grammar and varied sentence structure. Convey ideas clearly by organizing the essay properly. Usually a point by point or line by line analysis is effective.

The Essay - Literature and Composition

The Three Essays

The three forty minute essays on the Literature and Composition Exam usually follow a consistent pattern: one question on a passage of prose, one question on a poem, and one question on a work freely chosen by the student (usually called the "open" question). One variation may occur. Instead of writing on one passage or poem, the student may be asked to contrast two passages or two poems. Many of the passage analysis strategies used in the Language and Composition portion of the essay test can be applied to the prose and poetry questions of the Literature and Composition essay test with some modification. The free choice essay, however, emphasizes more of the literary aspects of literature.

The Open Question

Since the free choice asks the writer to select a distinguished novel or play to use as evidence to answer the question, students need to preview previously read literature in terms of their literary merit, in case this literature may be appropriate to use. Extensive reading from the list of suggested authors on pp. 3 - 5 of *A Practical Guide to the AP English Litera-ture and Composition Examination* is also recommended. The following is a generic composite of the types of free-choice (open) questions asked since 1970. These open questions have been divided into the basic elements of fiction: plot/conflict, setting, characterization, narration, theme, and style. Many are followed by quotes from works of literary merit that show some application for the question.

Applying these questions to the reading of any novel or play assigned can improve your critical thinking skills and increase your chance to score higher on the AP exam.

Plot/Conflict: In a selected work of literary merit, show, explain or demonstrate how . . .

1. The author reveals a character's unwillingness or inability to act through such elements of fiction as theme, symbol, set-ting, image, characterization, or other aspects of the narrative artist's craft.

> A. *A Woman of No Importance* by Oscar Wilde: "She loved him -- before the child was born -- for she had a child. She implored him for the child's sake to marry her, that the child might have a name, that her sin might not be visited on the child, who was in-nocent. He refused."
> B. *Mansfield Park* by Jane Austen: "She had more fears of her perseverance to remove . . . ill-nature -- selfishness -- and a fear of exposing herself"
> C. *The Old Man and the Sea* by Ernest Hemingway:
> D. *For Whom the Bell Tolls* by Ernest Hemingway:
> E. *Lucy Gayheart* by Willa Cather:
> F?

2. Any implausible or strikingly unrealistic incident or character, if evident, is related to the more realistic or plausible elements in the rest of the work.

    A. *The Scarlet Letter* by Nathaniel Hawthorne: "Not a stitch in that embroidered letter, but she had felt in her heart."

    C. *Maggie: A Girl of the Streets* by Stephen Crane: "The girl, Maggie, blossomed in a mud puddle. She grew to be a most rare and wonderful production of the tenement district, a pretty girl. None of the dirt of Rum Alley seemed to be in her veins. The philosophers upstairs, downstairs and on the same floor, puzzled over it."

    D. *Things Fall Apart* by Chinua Achebe: "Every clan and village had its 'evil forest.' In it were buried all those who died of the really evil diseases, like leprosy and small pox. It was also the dumping ground for potent fetishes of great medicine men when they died. An evil forest was, therefore, alive with sinister forces and powers of darkness."

    E. *A Tale of Two Cities* by Charles Dickens: "'Twas a blank and bleary, yet most frivolous night, when we first began our venture down Dead Man's Path through the heart of evil. Suddenly a wretched voice set out of the hills and raised the hair on our bodies. So horrible was the sound that many ran away in fear of being eaten."

    F. *My Antonia* by Willa Cather

    G?

3. Some works create a significant conflict between a parent (or a parental figure) and a son or daughter. Analyze the sources of the conflict and explain how the conflict contributes to the meaning of the work.

    A. *Washington Square* by Henry James: "I want to marry Morris, but if I do, it will disappoint my father greatly."

    B. *Maggie: A Girl of the Streets* by Stephen Crane: "Here, you Jim, git up, now, while I belt yer life out, you damned disorderly brat."

C. *Things Fall Apart* by Chinua Achebe: "Okonkwo
did not have the start in life which many young men
usually had. He did not inherit a barn from his father. There was no barn to inherit."
D. *The Color Purple* by Alice Walker:
E?

4. Writers who get the best response are writers who offer a
happy ending through moral development . . . some kind of
spiritual reassessment or moral reconciliation, even with the
self, even at death.
   A. *The Adventures of Huckleberry Finn* by Mark Twain
   B. *The Color Purple* by Alice Walker
   C. *Crime and Punishment* by Dostoevsky
   D. *Great Expectations* by Charles Dickens
   E. *A Doll's House* by Ibsen

Setting: In a selected work of literary merit, show, explain
or demonstrate how . . .

5. Some moments or scenes are especially memorable. Select
a line or so of poetry, or a moment or scene in a novel, or play
that you find especially memorable. Identify the line of passage; explain its relationship to the work in which it is found;
and analyze the reason for its effectiveness.
   A. *The Secret Agent* by Joseph Conrad: "Before reaching Knightsbridge, Mr. Verloc took a turn to the left
   out of the busy main thorouhfare, uproarious with
   the traffic of omnibuses and trotting vans, into the
   almost silent, swift flow of hansoms."
   B. *Maggie: A Girl of the Streets* by Stephen Crane:
   "Long streamers of garments fluttered from fire es-
   capes. In all unhandy places there were buckets,
   brooms, rags, and bottles. In the street infants played
   or fought with other infants or sat stupidly in the way
   of vehicles. Formidable woman, with uncombed hair
   and disordered dress, gossiped while leaning on rail-
   ings, or screamed in frantic quarrels. Withered
   persons, in curious postures of submission to something, sat smoking pipes in obscure corners. A thousand odors of cooking food came forth to the street.
   The building quivered and creaked from the weight
   of humanity stamping about in its bowels."

    C. *A Tale of Two Cities* by Charles Dickens: "It was the best of times, it was the worst of times, it was the age of wisdom, it was the age of foolishness, it was the epoch of belief, it was the epic of incredulity, it was the season of light, it was the season of darkness, it was the spring of hope, it was the winter of despair, we had everything before us, we had nothing before us, we were all going to heaven, we were all going the other way . . . ."

    D. *For Whom the bell Tolls* by Ernest Hemingway:

    E. *The Old Man and the Sea* by Ernest Hemingway:

    F?

6. Many plays and novels use contrasting places (for example, two countries, two cities, or towns, two houses, or the land and the sea) to represent opposed forces or ideas which are central to the meaning of the work. Select a work of literary merit that contrasts two places, explaining how the places differ, what each place represents, and how their contrasts contribute to the meaning of the work.

    A. *A Woman of No Importance* by Oscar Wilde: "We have the largest country in the world, Lady Caroline They used to tell us at school that some of our states are as big as France and England put together."

    B. *Lucy Gayheart* by Willa Cather:

    C. *The Color Purple* by Alice Walker:

    D?

Characterization: In a selected work of literary merit, show, explain or demonstrate how . . .

7. Two characters are portrayed as being naturally or unnaturally suited for one another.

    A. *The Turn of the Screw* by Henry James: "He knew me as well as I knew him; and so, in the cold, faint twilight, with a glimmer in the high glass and another on the polish of the oak stair below, we faced each other in our common intensity."."

    B. *The Bellarosa Connection* by Saul Bellow:

    C. *My Antonia* by Willa Cather:

    D?

8. Characters are always portrayed as being affected by and responding to the standards of a society. Describe the standards of the society in which the character exists, and show how the character is affected by and responds to the standards.

A. *A Woman of No Importance* by Oscar Wilde: "Well, you couldn't come to a more charming place than this, Miss Worsley, though the house is excessively damp, unpardonably damp, and dear Lady Hunstanton is sometimes a little lax about the people she asks down here."

B. *The House of Seven Gables* by Nathaniel Hawthorne: "Her new experience has led our decayed gentlewoman to very disagreeable conclusions as to the temper and manners of what was termed the lower class, whom heretofore she had looked down upon with a gentle and pitying complaisance, as herself occupying a sphere of unquestionable superiority."

C. *The Color Purple* by Alice Walker:

D?

9. The stereotyped character is employed successfully to achieve the author's purpose.

A. *Tar Baby* by Toni Morrison:

B. *The Adventures of Huckleberry Finn* by Mark Twain

C. *A Doll's House* by Ibsen

D. *A Street Car Named Desire* by Tennessee Williams

E?

10. The full presentation of a complex character in the work, whose actions alone define him as evil or immoral, makes us react more sympathetically than we otherwise might. This villain, also, always enhances the meaning of the work.

    A. *The Secret Agent* by Joseph Conrad: Mr. Verloc: "I don't want to look at you as long as I live."

    B. *The Grapes of Wrath* by John Steinbeck:

    C. *The Adventures of Huckleberry Finn* by Mark Twain

    D?

11. One of the characters is always a confidant (male) or confidante (female), often a friend or relative of the hero or heroine, whose role is to be present when the hero or heroine needs a sympathetic listener to confide in. However, the author sometimes uses this character for other purposes as well. Choose a confidant or confidante from a novel or play and discuss the various ways this character functions in the work.

    A. *Washington Square* by Henry James: "Mrs. Penniman smiled very sweetly as if she understood everything, and she made no attempt to contradict her."

    B?

12. A character who appears briefly, or does not appear at all, is a significant presence who affects action, theme, or the development of other characters.

    A. *Maggie: A Girl of the Streets* by Stephen Crane: "The babe, Tommy, died. He went away in a white, insignificant coffin, his small waxen hand clutching a flower that the girl, Maggie, had stolen from an Italian."

    B?

13. Writers often highlight the values of a culture or a society by using characters who are alienated from that culture or society because of gender, race, class or creed. This alienation always reveals something about the surrounding society's assumptions and moral values.

    A. The Scarlet Letter by Nathaniel Hawthorne: "Hester set forth to the place appointed for her punishment (a scaffold). This scaffold constituted a portion of a penal machine which . . . was held, in the old time, to be as effectual an agent, in the promotion of good citizenship, as ever was the guillotine among the terrorists of France. It was, in short, the platform of the pillory; and above it rose the framework of that instrument of discipline, so fashioned as to confine the human head in its tight grasp, and thus holding it up to the public gaze. The very ideal of ignominy was embodied and made manifest in this contrivance of wood and iron."
    B?

Narration: In a selected work of literary merit, show, explain or demonstrate how . . .

14. The element of time is used in a distinct way. The chronological sequence of events may be altered, or time may be suspended, or altered . . . contributing to the effectiveness of the work as a whole.

    A. *The Turn of the Screw* by Henry James: "At this point I precipitately found myself aware of three things. They were practically simultaneous, yet they had flashes of succession."
    B. *Lucy Gayheart* by Willa Cather: (The entire novel is a flashback.)
    C. *My Antonia* by Willa Cather:
    D?

15. Some of the most significant events are always mental or psychological; for example, awakenings, discoveries, changes in consciousness. Describe how the author of a work of literary merit gives these internal events the sense of excitement, suspense, and climax usually associated with external action.

A. *The Old man and the Sea* by Ernest Hemingway:

B. *The Secret Agent* by Joseph Conrad: "The prospect of having to break the news to her had put him in a fever. Chief Inspector Heat had relieved him of that task. . . . . It remained now for him to face her grief."

C?

Theme: In a selected work of literary merit, show, explain or demonstrate how . . .

16. Limitations of some aspect of contemporary society are reflected in a selected work of literary merit.

A. *A Woman of No Importance* by Oscar Wilde: "Only two kinds of society: the plain and the colored."

B?

17. The opening scene of a drama or the first chapter of a novel introduces some of the major themes of the work.

A. *The Old man and the Sea* by Ernest Hemingway

B. *The Scarlet Letter* by Nathaniel Hawthorne: "Before this ugly edifice, and between it and the wheel track of the street, was a grass plot, much overgrown with burdock, pigweed, appleperu, and such unsightly vegetation, which evidently found something congenial in the soil that had so early borne the black flower of civilized society, a prison."

C?

18. A selected work of literary merit, although written before 1900, has relevance for a person today.

A?

B?

19. A character exists who has a misconception of himself or his world. Show how destroying or perpetuating this illusion contributes to the central theme of the play.

A?

B?

20. The conflict created when the will of an individual opposes the will of the majority is a recurring theme. Analyze the conflict seen in your work and discuss the moral and ethical implications for both the individual and society.

    A?

    B?

21. A character's attempt to recapture or reject the past is an important theme in many plays, novels and poems. Choose a work in which a character views the past with such feelings as reverence, bitterness, or longing. Show with clear evidence how the character's view of the past is used to develop a theme in the work.

    A. *The Secret Agent* by Joseph Conrad: "You'll have to pull yourself together, my girl," he said, sympathetically. "What's done can't be undone."

    B. *My Antonia* by Willa Cather:

22. A recurring theme may also be the classic war between passion and responsibility. For instance, a personal cause, a love, a desire for revenge, a determination to redress a wrong, or some other emotion or drive may conflict with moral duty. Choose a literary work in which the character confronts the demands of a private passion that conflicts with his/her responsibilities. Show clearly the nature of the conflict, its affect upon the character, and the significance to the work.

    A. *For Whom the Bell Tolls* by Ernest Hemingway:

    B. *Tar Baby* by Toni Morrison:

23. Some works of literary merit seem to advocate changes in social or political attitudes or in traditions. Choose a novel or play and note briefly the particular attitudes or traditions that the author apparently wishes to modify. Then analyze the techniques the author uses to influence the reader's or audience's views.

    A?

    B?

Style: In a selected work of literary merit, show, explain or demonstrate how . . .

24. The title has significance that is developed through the author's use of devices such as contrast, repetition, allusion, and point of view.

    A. *The Secret Agent* by Joseph Conrad: "Night, the inevitable reward of man's faithful labors on this earth, night had fallen on Mr. Verloc, the tired revolutionist — 'one of the old lot' — the humble guardian of society; the invaluable **secret agent** . . . a servant of law and order, faithful, trusted, accurate, admirable, with perhaps one single amiable weakness: the idealistic belief of being loved for himself."

    B?

25. Each author's presentation of details (word choice, imagery, phrasing, and sentence structure) is intended to shape the reader's attitudes toward the place or person he describes.

    A. *A Woman of No Importance* by Oscar Wilde: "To get into the best society, nowadays, one either has to feed people, amuse people, or shock people — that is all."

    B. *The Turn of the Screw* by Henry James: "My candle, under a bold flourish, went out, and I perceived, by the uncovered window, that the yielding dusk of earliest morning rendered it unnecessary."

    C. *The Scarlet Letter* by Nathaniel Hawthorne: "Stretching forth the official staff in his left hand, he laid his right upon the shoulder of a woman, whom he thus drew forward; until, on the threshold of the prison door, she repelled him by an action marked with natural dignity and force of character, and stepped into the open air, as if by her own free will."

    D?

26. The ending appropriately or inapprorpiately concludes the work.

    A. *The House of Seven Gables* by Nathaniel Hawthorne: "Maules Well, all this time, though left in solitude, was throwing up a succession of kaleidoscopic pictures in which a gifted eye might have foreshadowed

the coming fortunes of . . . ."
B?

27. The meaning of some literary works is often enhanced by sustained allusions to myths, the Bible, or other works of literature. Select a literary work that makes use of a sustained reference. Expalin the allusion that predominates the work and analyze how it enhances the work's meaning.
 A. *Tar Baby* by Toni Morrison:
 B?

28. The audience is confronted with a scene or scenes of violence which contribute to the meaning of the complete work.
 A. *Native Son* by Richard Wright: "
 B. *Maggie: A Girl of the Streets* by Stephen Crane: "
 C?

29. One important measure of a superior work of literature is its ability to produce in the reader a healthy confusion of pleasure and disquietude. Select a work that produces this healthy confusion. Explain the sources of the pleasure and disquietude experienced by the reader of the work.
 A?
 B?

30. Some works have a blend of humor, pathos, and the grotesque.
 A. *Maggie: A Girl of the Streets* by Stephen Crane: "Once, when a lady had dropped her purse on the sidewalk, the gnarled and leathery woman had grabbed it and smuggled it with great dexterity beneath her cloak. When she was arrested she cursed the lady in a partial swoon, and with her aged limbs, twisted from rheumatism, had almost kicked the stomach out of a huge policeman whose conduct she referred to when she said: "The police, damn 'em."

 A?
 B?

31. Some works make a good case for distortion as a way of making people see.

>A. *The Scarlet Letter* by Nathaniel Hawthorne: The Scarlet Letter "had the effect of a spell, taking her out of the ordinary relations with humanity, and enclosing her in a sphere within herself."
>
>B?

32. Sometimes "a scene or character awakens 'thoughtful laughter' in the reader.

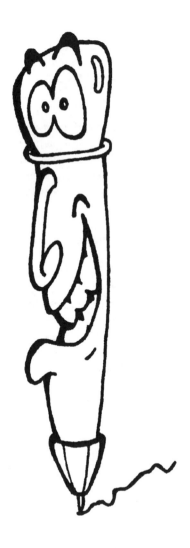

The Essay - Literature and Composition
Typical Questions Chart

PREFACE:

The following chart shows what type of AP English Literature questions were asked each year. The following titles are used to signify the type of question asked: **Attitude (Also known as** tone, attitude, or point of view), **Effect,** Literary Effects (referred to as **Plot, Conflict, Setting, Character, Narration, Theme, or Style**), and **Meaning.** Comparison/Contrast Questions are referred to as **CC(. . .).**

Year	Prose	Poetry	Open
1970	Character	Attitude	Character
1971	Attitude	Theme	Style
1972	Character	No Poem Attitude Essay	Conflict
1973	CC(Attitude)	No Poem Attitude Essay	Style
1974	No Prose	Attitude	Theme
1975	Plot	No Poetry Open(Narration)	Character
1976	Effect	Attitude	Theme
1977	No Prose	CC(Style)	Theme
1978	Attitude	Meaning	Plot

Year	Prose	Poetry	Open
1979	Attitude	CC(Attitude)	Character
1980	CC(Attitude/ Effect)	Attitude	Theme
1981	Attitude	Meaning	Style
1982	No Prose Argument	Attitude	Style
1983	Attitude	Attitude	Setting
1984	Effect	No Poetry Character	Style
1985	CC(Effect)	CC(Attitude)	Style
1986	Attitude	Tone& Meaning	Narration
1987	Attitude	Attitude	Theme
1988	Effect	CC(Theme& Style)	Narration
1989	Attitude	Meaning	Style
1990	Attitude	Attitude	Conflict
1991	CC(Attitude)	Attitude	Setting
1992	Attitude	Attitude	Character
1993	Attitude	Meaning	Style
1994	Dramatizing	CC(Attitude)	Character
1995	Character	Attitude	Character
1996	Character	Attitude	Plot

The Essay - Literature and Composition

Comparison/ Contrast Questions

The following questions can be used to write a comparison/ contrast essay between two works or two passages:

1. In the following two passages, both author's seem to portray their character as ____. In a well-organized essay, analyze how each author uses imagery, diction, and descriptive language to illustrate different aspects of ____.

2. The speaker in both pasages below is describing a ____. After reading both passages, analyze how each author uses language differently to portray the speaker's attitude toward his/her ____.

3. The following passages show characters who have contrasting views of ____. Read these passsages, then show how each author uses vivid details, selective diction, and similies to portray the different views.

4. The following two poems discuss the importance of ____. Read the poems. Then write an essay demonstrating how this importance is displayed differently through the use of diction, imagery, and sound devices.

5. In the following passages, each character is running away from ____. Read the passages carefully. Then write a well-organized essay in which you describe the author's attitude toward how the character deals with his/her ____.

6. Discuss _____ as a recurring motif in each of the passages. Analyze how the language affects the character's attitude.

7. The passages below deal with less than average _____ role models. How do the similar language devices displayed reveal different aspects of each character's disgrace?

8. In the passages below, each character is displaying dispicable behavior. Analyze how each author uses similar rhetorical and stylistics devices to reveal differnt levels of disapproval toward these character's actions.

9. The characters in the following passages are involved in similar conflicts. How does each author use such devices as imagery, descriptive diction, and allusions to make the conflicts seem real to the reader?

10. The passages below deal with two villians (or heroes). After reading each passage carefully, write an essay in which you analyze how each narrator presents these villains (or heroes). Consider such rhetorical features as tone, imagery, and effect.

11. In the following passages, both characters are being judged by an _____ on the subject of _____. Read the passages carefully. Then write a well-organized essay describing how each author uses literary devices to portray the _____' attitudes toward _____.

12. In the following poems, both characters show a change in attitude. After carefully reading these passages, analyze the language devices used to illustrate this change.

The Essay

Student Grading
Made Easy With
Comprehensive
Checklists:

Each essay question written by Advanced Placement is graded by a set of Rubrics. Sample Rubrics are available through *The Advanced Placement Program: The College Board*. Examining these rubrics, I discovered that they addressed 9 separate categories. Designing a checklist with 9 items to arrive at a score out of 9 is a result of this discovery. I use the checklists in the following ways:

New Learning:

These checklists are designed to help students understand what is expected by AP for each type of question. When introducing a new type of essay, I refer them to the appropriate checklist on pages 40 - 51 and discuss its content. This prepares them for effective writing by making them familiar with the AP expectations for that particular essay. I then have them apply those checklists to writing an AP essay on that type of question. Becoming familiar with what is expected by AP for each type of question helps the student read more critically and write more maturely.

Student Grading:

These checklists are also designed to help students grade each others essays. These checklists make the grading as objective and easy as possible. After completing any practice essay assigned, I usually have students from a different AP section grade these anonymously using the checklist that would apply to that question. They do this by filling out a generic cover sheet using the proper checklist in this chapter as a guide. This provides student feedback that can be used in conferencing (See "Checklist Cover Sheet" on next page).

Multiple Conferencing:

Perhaps the best feature of the checklists is that they demand dialogue among the learners. I grade the essays holistically, placing a pencilled mark out of 9 in my grade book. If my mark varies more than 2 points from the combined results of the two graders, I conference with them. Once students get their results back, they are required to record their grades with me. Here they are allowed to negotiate for a higher grade if they can adequately defend their writing. More learning about writing takes place here than has ever happened before for me.

Reinforced Learning:

The checklists can also be used as a question recognition check. Once all the types of questions are taught in steps 1 - 3, we still read continuously. Occasionally I will write an AP question on the board that addresses this reading. Then I have them write the essay in one class period. At the end of the period they take a "Checklist Cover Sheet," placing the correct name of the type of essay on the top and turn this in when its ready to grade. Picking the right checklist from pages 40 - 51 helps them recognize the requirements of the question. For instance, if they define the meaning of the passage instead of the speaker's attitude, they have not answered the question and, even though their essay may be maturely written, they will receive a low score because they did not answer the question.

Use the Checklist Cover Sheet on the next two pages in conjunction with the complete checklists that follow.

The Essay Checklist for:

_____

Student Writer Name   -   Class Period

_____

Type of Essay

from _____

(Author - *Title*)

STEP 1: Subtract one point for each item **not checked** from the checklist below:

___-___1.   GRADER RESPONSE:

___-___2.

___-___3.

___-___4.

___-___5.

___-___6.

___-___7.

___-___8.

___-___9.

MAXIMUM SCORE RESULTS: Grader 1 _____

MAXIMUM SCORE RESULTS: Grader 2 _____

STEP 2: Subtract one point from the results of step 1 for each item **checked** from the rubrics list below. NOTE: To avoid a negative number, you may not have any more checks here than the total on the left.

___-__1.   GRADER RESPONSE:

___-__2.

___-__3.

___-__4.

___-__5.

___-__6.

___-__7.

___-__8.

___-__9.

RESULTS:

Grader 1: _____ - _____ = _____
                  Step 1 Score   Step 2 Score

Grader 2: _____ - _____ = _____
                  Step 1 Score   Step 2 Score

Grader 1 Score + Grader 2 Score = _____

Above sum
divided by 2 =

Score for essay

The Essay-- Checklist for Tone, POV, or Attitude

Step One: Add one point for each item checked from the list. (Grader one should check column 1. Grader 2 should check column 2):

___-___1. The essay demonstrates an understanding of the author's (speaker's or character's) complex attitude.

___-___2. The essay analyzes how literary, stylistic, or narrative devices listed in the question or used in the passage or poem distinguish the complexity of the author's (speaker's or character's) attitude.

___-___3. The essay offers a convincing interpretation of the passage or poem.
.

___-___4. The writer's use of quotes shows an appreciation of the author's (poet's) style.

___-___5. The writer's explanations of the evidence are clear, concise and consistent with the meaning of the passage.

___-___6. This essay supports the discussion of each language device with apt and specific references to the text.

___-___7. The diction / sentence structure of this essay communicates a clear message.

___-___8. The implicit organization of this essay aids in communicating a clear message.

___-___9. The grammar aids in communicating a clear message.

MAXIMUM SCORE RESULTS: Grader 1 _____

MAXIMUM SCORE RESULTS: Grader 2 _____

STEP 2: Subtract one point from the results of step 1 for each item **checked** from the rubrics list below. NOTE: To avoid a negative number, you may not have any more checks here than the total on the left.

___-___1. The essay's discussion of the author's (speaker's or character's) complex view is less incisive than those of the highest scoring essays.

___-___2. The writer discusses the literary, stylistic, or narrative devices with limited purpose or accuracy.

___-___3. The essay's interpretation of the passage or poem may be vague or pedestrian or incorrect.

___-___4. The writer's use of quotes is awkward, inappropriate, or uninteresting.

___-___5. The writer simply catalogues the rhetorical or stylistic devices without relating them to the creation of the author's (Speaker's or character's) attitude.

___-___6. Although adequate in number, the evidence in this essay is not as thorough or precise as the top-scoring essays.

___-___7. Distracting errors in diction, or syntax make the message unclear.

___-___8. The organization of this essay is less appropriate than those of the top-scoring essays.

___-___9. The essay reveals consistent weakness in grammar and/or other basic elements of composition.

RESULTS:

Grader 1: _____ - _____ = _____
    Step 1 Score   Step 2 Score

Grader 2: _____ - _____ = _____
    Step 1 Score   Step 2 Score

Grader 1 Score + Grader 2 Score = _____

Above sum divided by 2 =

Score for essay

The Essay-- Checklist for Effect

Step One: Add one point for each item checked from the list. (Grader one should check column 1. Grader 2 should check column 2):

___-___1. The essay comments on the probable or intended effect of the passage with psychological insight.

___-___2. The essay analyzes how all the literary, narrative, or stylistic devices listed in the question or used in the passage define the author's probable or intended effect.

___-___3. These essays show an excellent appreciation of the contextual relationships of the passage.

___-___4. This essay is written in an appropriate and interesting format.

___-___5. The thesis clearly shows the connection between the author's probable or intended effect and the language devices used to create that effect.

___-___6. This essay persuasively substantiates the discussion of each language device with a minimum of three embedded bits of quotes per paragraph.

___-___7. The diction / sentence structure of this essay communicates an understandable message.

___-___8. The ideas in this essay are expressed in an ordered or logical sequence.

___-___9. The grammar aids in communicating a clear message.

MAXIMUM SCORE RESULTS: Grader 1 _____

MAXIMUM SCORE RESULTS: Grader 2 _____

STEP 2: Subtract one point from the results of step 1 for each item **checked** from the rubrics list below. NOTE: To avoid a negative number, you may not have any more checks here than the total on the left.

___-___1. The writer comments on the intended or probable effects in ways not supported by the text.

___-___2. The writer discusses the rhetorical and stylistic strategies with limited purpose or accuracy.

___-___3. The writer simply paraphrases the content of the passage.

___-___4. The writer simply catalogues the rhetorical or stylistic devices without relating them to the creation of the author's effect.

___-___5. The connection between the evidence and the author's purpose is less clear than those of the top-scoring essays.

___-___6. Although adequate in number, the evidence in this essay is not as convincing as the top-scoring essay.

___-___7. A few lapses in diction, or syntax may be present, but the message is clear.

___-___8. The organization of this essay is less appropriate than those of the top-scoring essays.

___-___9. The essay reveals consistent weakness in grammar and/or other basic elements of composition.

RESULTS:

Grader 1: _____ - _____ = _____
          Step 1 Score   Step 2 Score

Grader 2: _____ - _____ = _____
          Step 1 Score   Step 2 Score

Grader 1 Score + Grader 2 Score = _____

Above sum divided by 2 =

Score for essay

 **The Essay**-- Checklist for
Literary Elements

Step One: Add one point for each item checked from the list.
(Grader one should check column 1. Grader 2 should check
column 2):

___-___1. These essays demonstrate an understanding of how
the author reveals character, plot/conflict, setting, or theme.

___-___2. The essay analyzes how all the literary, narrative,
or stylistic devices listed in the question or used in the passage
capture the intensity of the character, plot/conflict, setting, or
theme.

___-___3. These essays recognize the complexity of the author's
characterization, plot/conflict, setting, or theme.

___-___4. This essay presents an individual understanding of
the text.

___-___5. The thesis clearly shows the connection between the
author's language and the creation of character, plot/conflict,
setting, or theme.
___-___6. This essay persuasively substantiates the discussion
of each language device with a minimum of three embedded
bits of quotes per paragraph.

___-___7. The diction / sentence structure of this essay communicates an understandable message.

___-___8. The ideas in this essay are expressed in an ordered
or logical sequence.

___-___9. The grammar aids in communicating a clear message.
  MAXIMUM SCORE RESULTS: Grader 1 _____

MAXIMUM SCORE RESULTS: Grader 2 _____

STEP 2: Subtract one point from the results of step 1 for each item **checked** from the rubrics list below. NOTE: To avoid a negative number, you may not have any more checks here than the total on the left.

___-___1. These writer's understanding of how the author reveals character, plot/conflict, setting, or theme is vague, mechanical, or overly generalized.

___-___2. The writer discusses the literary and stylistic strategies with limited purpose or accuracy.

___-___3. The writer simply paraphrases the content of the passage or says nothing beyond the easy and obvious to grasp.

___-___4. The essay reflects an incomplete understanding of the story and fails to respond adequately to the question.

___-___5. The discussion of how the author uses the language is misguided, inaccurate, or unclear.

___-___6. Although adequate in number, the evidence in this essay is not as convincing as the top-scoring essay.

___-___7. A few lapses in diction, or syntax may be present, but the message is clear.

___-___8. The organization of this essay is less appropriate than those of the top-scoring essays.

___-___9. The essay reveals consistent weakness in grammar and/or other basic elements of composition.

RESULTS:

Grader 1: _____ - _____ = _____

        Step 1 Score   Step 2 Score

Grader 2: _____ - _____ = _____

        Step 1 Score   Step 2 Score

Grader 1 Score + Grader 2 Score = _____

Above sum divided by 2 =

Score for essay

 # Checklist for Comparison/ Contrast Essay

Step One: Add one point for each item checked from the list. (Grader one should check column 1. Grader 2 should check column 2):

___-___1. The attitude, effect, or meaning defined demonstrates a perceptive insight into each of the works.

___-___2. The essay shows how all of the literary or stylistic devices seen in both passages are used differently to create an attitude, effect or meaning.

___-___3. This writer has reached valid, pertinent, and relevant conclusions about the comparison.

___-___4. This writer has shown an appreciation of the contextual relationship between the two excerpts.

___-___5. The thesis clearly shows the connection between the author's (or Poet's) attitude, effect or meaning and the language devices used to convey that attitude.

___-___6. This essay supports the discussion of each language device with good and persuasive substantiation of both works (a minimum of three embedded bits of quotes per paragraph).

___-___7. The diction / sentence structure of this essay communicates a clear message.

___-___8. The organization of this essay aids in communicating a clear message.

___-___9. The grammar aids in communicating a clear message.

MAXIMUM SCORE RESULTS: Grader 1 _____

MAXIMUM SCORE RESULTS: Grader 2 _____

STEP 2: Subtract one point from the results of step 1 for each item **checked** from the rubrics list below. NOTE: To avoid a negative number, you may not have any more checks here than the total on the left.

____-____1. The writer simply names the probable or intended attitude, effect, or meaning (or the three devices, or both) with no discussion.

____-____2. The writer discusses the literary and stylistic strategies with limited purpose or accuracy.

____-____3. The writer simply paraphrases each passage.

____-____4. The writer simply catalogues the rhetorical or stylistic devices without relating them to the creation of the authors' probable or intended attitude, effect, or meaning .

____-____5. The connection between the evidence and the authors' probable or intended attitude, effect, or meaning is less clear than those of the top-scoring essays.

____-____6. Although adequate in number, the evidence in this essay is not as convincing as the top-scoring essay.

____-____7. A few lapses in grammar, diction, or syntax may be present, but the message is clear.

____-____8. The organization of this essay is less appropriate than those of the top-scoring essays.

____-____9. The essay reveals consistent weakness in grammar and/or other basic elements of composition.

RESULTS:

Grader 1: _____ - _____ = _____
                    Step 1 Score   Step 2 Score

Grader 2: _____ - _____ = _____
                    Step 1 Score   Step 2 Score

Grader 1 Score + Grader 2 Score = _____

Above sum divided by 2 =

Score for essay

Checklist for Essays on Meaning

Step One: Add one point for each item checked from the list. (Grader one should check column 1. Grader 2 should check column 2):

___-___1. This essay clearly demonstrates an understanding of the poem's (passage's) literal and figurative meanings.

___-___2. This essay discusses how the language, structure, and imagery of the poem (or passage) are used to convey meaning.

___-___3. This essay supports the discussion of each language device with apt and specific evidence.

___-___4. This writer recognizes the multiple perspectives seen in the poem (or passage).

___-___5. This paper offers a convincing interpretation of the poem (or passage).

___-___6. The writer demonstrates an ability to read perceptively by saying something beyond the easy and obvious to grasp.

___-___7. The diction / sentence structure of this essay communicates a clear message.

___-___8. The organization of this essay aids in communicating a clear message.

___-___9. The grammar aids in communicating a clear message.

MAXIMUM SCORE RESULTS: Grader 1 _____

MAXIMUM SCORE RESULTS: Grader 2 _____

STEP 2: Subtract one point from the results of step 1 for each item **checked** from the rubrics list below. NOTE: To avoid a negative number, you may not have any more checks here than the total on the left.

___-___1. This essay's definition of the poem's (passage's) meaning is less thorough or less precise than those of the highest scoring essays .

___-___2. This essay's discussion of language, structure, and imagery is briefer and less incisive than those of the highest scoring essays.

___-___3. This essay's discussion of language, structure, and imagery is less well-developed that the best papers.

___-___4. This writer misses the complexity of meaning that the poem (or passage) describes.

___-___5. This paper fails to respond to part(s) of the question.

___-___6. The discussion of meaning may be pedestrian, inaccurate or unclear.

___-___7. A few lapses in diction, or syntax may be present, but the message is clear.

___-___8. The organization of this essay is less appropriate than those of the top-scoring essays.

___-___9. The essay reveals consistent weakness in grammar and/or other basic elements of composition.

RESULTS:

Grader 1: _____ - _____ = _____
        Step 1 Score   Step 2 Score

Grader 2: _____ - _____ = _____
        Step 1 Score   Step 2 Score

Grader 1 Score + Grader 2 Score = _____

Above sum divided by 2 =

Score for essay

Checklist for the "Open" or "Free-Choice" Essay

Step One: Add one point for each item checked from the list. (Grader one should check column 1. Grader 2 should check column 2):

___-___1. The writer selects a suitable novel or play in which the literary element addressed in the question is significant to the work as a whole.
___-___2. The writer presents a reasonable explanation of the purpose and meaning of the work.

___-___3. The writer effectively establishes how the literary element addressed in the question is significant to the work as a whole..
___-___4. The writer effectively explains how the literary element is significant to the work as a whole..

___-___5. The writer makes apt and specific reference to the text.
___-___6. The writer avoids plot summary not relevant to the explanation of the significant literary element.

___-___7. The writer discusses the literary work with sophistication, insight, and understanding.

___-___8. The writer's displays consistent control over the language unique to the discussion of literature.

___-___9. The writer's diction, sentence structure, organization, and grammar aid in communicating a clear message.

MAXIMUM SCORE RESULTS: Grader 1 _____

MAXIMUM SCORE RESULTS: Grader 2 _____

STEP 2: Subtract one point from the results of step 1 for each item **checked** from the rubrics list below. NOTE: To avoid a negative number, you may not have any more checks here than the total on the left.

___-___1. The writer's selection of a work of literary merit is not as appropriate as those of the higher scoring essays.

___-___2. The writer's explanation of the meaning of the work is less thorough, less specific, or less perceptive than those of the higher scoring essays.

___-___3. The writer's explanation of the significance of the literary element addressed in the question may be vague, underdeveloped, or misguided.

___-___4. The writer's explanation of how the literary element is significant to the work as a whole may be less convincing, mechanical, or inadequately related to the work as a whole.

___-___5. The writer's reference to the text lack the specificity of the higher scoring essays.

___-___6. The writer simply paraphrases the meaning of the work with little reference to the significance of the literary element addressed in the question.

___-___7. The writer says nothing beyond the easy and obvious to grasp.

___-___8. The writer misuses the literary term(s) necessary to the discussion of literature or omits them partially or entirely.

___-___9. The essay contains distracting errors in grammar and mechanics.

RESULTS:

Grader 1: _____ - _____ = _____
       Step 1 Score   Step 2 Score

Grader 2: _____ - _____ = _____
       Step 1 Score   Step 2 Score

Grader 1 Score + Grader 2 Score = _____

Above sum /
divided by 2 =

Score for essay

AP Scoring
for Tests

54321

Student Name _____

The following represents a typical 2 - 3 week work load with typical AP conversions applied to arriving at a regular grade in the classroon.

Section I: Multiple-Choice:

_____ - (1/4 _____) X 1.35 = _____ (67.5)

Number	Number	Weighted	Max
Right out of 50	Wrong	Section I	Possible
		Score	

Section II:
Free-Response:

_____ + _____ + _____ X 3.0556 = _____(82.5012)

Essay 1	Essay 2	2 wk	Weighted Score	Max
(9 point scale)		Theme	Section II)	Possible

Test Composite Score:

_____ + _____ =

Weighted Section I	Weighted Section II	Composite Score
Score	Score	(out of 150)

AP Grade:

AP Grade Conversion:

150 - 107	(71%)	5	A
106 - 93	(62%)	4	B
92 - 74	(49%)	3	C
73 - 44	(29%)	2	D
43 - 0		1	F

AP Scoring
for Homework

54321

Section III:

_____ _____ / _____

Name of Homework Activity   My points   Points Possible

Section IV:

_____ _____ / _____

Name of Homework Activity   My points   Points Possible

Section V:

_____ _____ / _____

Name of Homework Activity   My points   Points Possible

Homework Total Points =

Homework Composite/Ap Score/Grade
Fill in the Curve

_____ - _____	(71%)	5	A
_____ - _____	(62%)	4	B
_____ - _____	(49%)	3	C
_____ - _____	29%)	2	D
_____ - _____		1	F

MY TOTALS:

_____ + _____ + _____ =

Previous   Test   Hmwk
Totals   Score   Score

My Grade=

Date=

(AP)   (Letter)

___ - ___ - ___

Write in curve below

_____ - _____	(71%)	5	A
_____ - _____	(62%)	4	B
_____ - _____	(49%)	3	C
_____ - _____	(29%)	2	D
_____ - _____		1	F

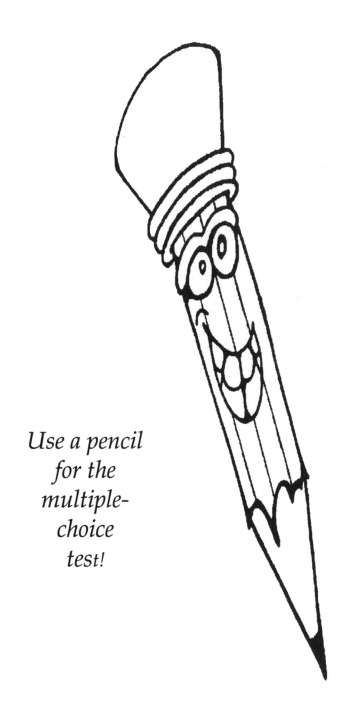

*Use a pencil
for the
multiple-
choice
test!*

Chapter Three: Multiple-Choice

Literature and Composition AP

Multiple-Choice

Test-taking
Strategies &
Suggestions

The multiple-choice section of the exam consists of 50 to 60 questions on four passages which have to be answered in one hour. Full length practice tests are included in this booklet. Take these under real test conditions, allowing no more than one hour to complete the exam. Practice some of the strategies below and adopt those which work for you.

1. Become familiar with the directions. Those listed below are the same ones as used on any AP multiple-choice exam.

> Directions: This part consists of selections from prose works and questions on their content, form and style. After reading each passage, choose the best answer to each question and completely fill in the corresponding oval on the answer sheet. Note: Pay particular attention to the requirement of the questions that contain the words NOT, LEAST, or EXCEPT.

2. Skim over each passage before beginning. The questions do not need to be completed in any certain order. If the first passage seems difficult, skip it, looking for the easiest passage. After answering those easier questions, go on and complete as much of the exam as time allows. Note: If you do not start in the beginning, make sure to mark the answers in the right number on the oval answer sheets. Perhaps a good strategy here would be to mark the answers in the test booklet and then mark the corresponding ovals on the answer sheet after completing the entire exam.

3. Once you've selected a passage to begin, skim through the questions (but not the choices) so you know what to expect. Then, read the passage actively, circle items that seem to be addressed in the questions.

4. After reading the passage, read the questions, crossing out the obviously wrong answers. An answer will be wrong if it:

> a. Contradicts the passage;

   b. Is irrelevant to the passage; or
   c. Is the same as one other choice and no
      choice allows you to pick both as the right
      answer.

Note: Since any marked answer that is wrong costs an additional .25, leave the question blank unless you can make an "educated guess."

5. The questions are asked in the order that they appear in the passage, rather than by difficulty. A good strategy here would be to mark where each question is addressed in the passage. This will save time because you know that the next question will be after that in the passage.

6. Read all the choices before making a decision. Avoid selecting an answer, only to find out later that an obviously better choice appeared later that you did not even read.

7. Learn how to paraphrase the author main ideas. Perhaps you will need to write the meaning down in the harder passages.

8. Manage your time by dividing each passage into 15 minute segments (4 passages X 15 minutes = One hour). If you are having trouble with an answer, eliminate the obviously wrong answer by crossing them out on the answer booklet, skip the question and come back later within the same 15 minute period. It is too time-consuming to have to rethink a question after reading another passage. Note: Be aware of the questions which include the words NOT, LEAST, or EXCEPT. In these cases, the right answer will be the one that does not apply to the passage.

9. See separate teacher's guide addendum for answers and explanations for all multiple-choice tests in this book. Correct your test, analyzing your mistakes to avoid similar patterns in the future.

Multiple-Choice

ABCDE

Collaborative
Writing
Directions

One of the best ways to learn how to score better on multiple-choice exams is to make multiple-choice exams. I have three AP sections so I have each section write one class test. Step One begins in the first week and the final product is completed at the end, 12 weeks later, and used as the final test.

Step One : Individual Journal Entry Assignment

Each member of the class finds four well-written expository, descriptive, narrative or persuasive passages from the AP suggested reading list in Chapter One. These excerpts should be written in the journal or word processed and submitted to the entire class for selection. One of the most effective ways to complete this assignment may be to surf the Internet. Many of these authors have home pages that can be quickly printed. Just type in their name on any search engine on Net Scape and you'll be surprised at your results.

Step Two: Collaborative Assignment

The class reads the excerpts submitted by its members. The top four submissions are selected based on their literary worth and appropriateness. Students are then selected to word process and photocopy the submissions selected for use in their class multiple choice test. The class is then divided into four passage groups, each group assigned the task to write 20 questions on their passage.

Step Three: Individual Journal Entry Assignment

Each member of the class writes a separate, brief critical analysis of each of the three passages not assigned to their small group. These are submitted to the small group designated to work on that passage.

Step Four: Collaborative Assignment

Reading the critical analyses submitted on their passage, each small group member takes notes on the critical analyses read, discussing their content and assigning types of questions to each member. These written questions must emphasize the same variety as seen in the AP Typical Questions on pp. 64 - 75. Each small group member is assigned specific types of questions so the final small group submission of 20 questions will reflect the variety required.

Step Five: Individual Journal Writing Assignment

Each member of the small group is assigned an equal amount of questions, but of the designated variety seen in the third number ratio in parentheses. One member might write 3 "vocabulary" questions and 2 "meaning" questions; another might write 2 "meaning" questions and 3 "dominant technique" questions, etc.

Step Six: Collaborative Assignment

The small group members share their results with their own group, selecting the top 12-15 for use in their class multiple choice test. These are then presented to the large group for acceptance. Note: Final selections of questions by the large group must reflect the variety indicated in the second number ratio in parentheses after each Typical Question on pp. 64 - 75. Students are then selected to word process the selected questions next to the already word processed and selected excerpts being used, arranging these questions in the order that they appear in the passage. When this is done the test has to be photocopied so that each member of the class can do the next step.

Step Seven: Individual Assignment

Each member of the class is assigned an equal number of questions on passages not written by his/her group. An explanation for each question's answer has to be written.

Step Eight: Collaborative Assignment

The class discusses the answers and explanations to the questions read by the individual that wrote them, agreeing on any final changes.

Step Nine: Individual Assignment

Each member of the class takes notes on the discussion of the rationale for the right answer for his/her assigned questions, revising their explanation for the answers. Students then are assigned to put these explanations together in the order they appear and photocopy them for distribution to the class that takes the test.

Step Ten: Collaborative Assignment

The class practices strategies listed on pp. 60 - 61 by taking the test written by another section, discussing the results when they are corrected, making changes where poorly written questions or choices warrant a different best answer.

The following paraphrasing of multiple-choice questions comes from the 1991 and 1994 *Advanced Placement Examination in English Literature and Composition and Its Grading* .

READING COMPREHENSION:

A. **Vocabulary:** Define words in context (1-2 out of 55)
>1. In line 26, "what's disjunct" refers to something that
>2. In context, " . . ." (line 23) is interpreted as
>3. In line 32, ". . ." is best interpreted as meaning

B. **Narration / Point of View:** Identify the speaker or the speaker's purpose OR attitude (4 out of 55)
>1. The point of view in the passage is that of a A. participating observer who is partial to someone B. Third person narrator who is aware of the main character's thoughts (central omniscient) C. Non-participating narrator who is unaware of the main character's thoughts (third person objective) D. First person narrator who refers of himself in the third person E. Third person narrator who reveals the thoughts of several characters (Omniscient).
>2. The narrator's attitude toward the main character can best be described as one of A. Pity B. Objectivity C. Sardonic condemnation D. Emotional Judgement E. Jaded disgust.
>3-4. The speaker of the passage is A. A resentful victim B. An unwelcome visitor C. An ironic commentator D. A curious investigator E. An apologetic participant.

C. **Pronoun/object reference:** (2-3 out of 55)
>1. In lines 28-29, the pronoun "it" in the phrase "it . . ." refers to (Choices are nouns in the passage).
>2. The object of "to" in line 32 is
>3. In line 32, "they" refers to
>4. In line 8, "its" refers to
>5. The antecedent of "them" in line 21 is

D. **Meaning: (12-15 out of 55)**
>1. It can be inferred from the phrase ". . ." (line 24) that the speaker A. Dreaded ___ B. Responded strongly but ambivalently to ___ C. Found the ___ in the ___ mystifying and unpleasant D. Was indifferent to the emotional force that lay behind the ___ E. Was dis-

turbed by the insincerity of ___.

2. The qualifiers "for them" and "so everyone said" suggests that the speaker A. Is confident that he will ___ B. Shares the experience of those around him sympathetically C. feels himself to be isolated from the rest of the people D. Views __ as the ultimate authority over himself E. is more interested in the experience of __ than that of ___.

3. In the context of the poem, the phrase ". . ." is best interpreted to mean . . .

4. Which of the following pairs of words refer to different entities?

5. When the speaker says that ". . . " he means that____

6. In the context of the poem, the phrase " . . ." is best interpreted to mean

7. Lines 14-17 describe an example of

8. In lines 20-21, " . . ." can be best paraphrased as

9. By the expression " . . ." the speaker means

10. In the first stanza, the whippoorwill is presented chiefly as A. a kind of poet B. A symbol of death C. An emblem of freedom D. An annoyance E. A messenger

11. ___ is most likely called "a voice of obsession" because

12. How many reasons does the speaker give to try to explain why ___?

13. The speaker hypothesizes that

14. For the speaker, the ___ and the ___ are both similar in that they

15. In line 25, the speaker implies that

16. Which of the following words is LEAST important to the theme of the poem?

17. The phrase ". . ." emphasizes which of the following?

18-19. In lines 23-30, the speaker implies that

20. The phrase ". . ." (line 6) emphasizes which of the following? A. The delicacy of the ___ B. The brain's ability to conceive C. The ___'s intuitive nature D. The feminine nature of the artist E. The need to be merciful.

21. The speakers thoughts are not comforting because

22. In line 18, ". . ." refers to the idea that

23. When ___ says "..." he means that

24. In the passage, ___ reflects on which of the following? A. Religion B. Other's misfortunes C. Escape D. Deposition E. Revenge.

25. Which of the following best restates the meaning

26. The speaker characterizes the life of the mountain village as A. Simple but rewarding B. Severe but patiently endured C. Enlightened by religion D. Wild as the surrounding landscape E. Cursed by both God and nature

27. Which of the following is the most logical deduction from the speaker's assertions?

E. Characterization: (6-7 out of 55)

1. Which of the following statements most pointedly refers to ___'s parsimonious character?

2-4. In the context of the sentence, the phrases "..." and "..." are used to show (what character trait)

5. Which of the following statements best defines ___'s relationship to ___? A. ___ is only devoted to ___ only out of a sense of moral obligation, ___ makes a display of loving ___ because of a debt he owes ___, ___ pretends to cherish ___ because he has designs on ___' inheritance, ___ is unwilling to accept ___ because he holds a grudge against ___'s mother, ___ treats ___ with disdain because he is jealous of ___.

6. Which of the following best describes the purpose of the last paragraph? A. It illustrates how ___' political and family affairs reflect his character B. It counters speculations about ___'s character C. It shows how ___'s shortcomings are beneficial to his career D. It introduces ___'s role as an observer of ___'s actions E. It suggests the causes of ___'s moral transformation.

7. The narrator attributes ___'s attitude and behavior to which of the following factors? A. Lack of formal education B. Absence of religious beliefs C. Traits of his ancestors D. Social rank and flawed character E. Unsuccessful marriage and unprofitable projects.

SOME CHARACTER TRAIT CHOICES INCLUDE:
haughty condescension, uninhibited passions, misguided optimism, awkwardness, duplicity, capacity for treachery, competent, respected, devoted to ___, competent, a servant of ___,

inadequately compensated, used his position for selfish ends, social and political astuteness, verbal and rhetorical facility, single-minded intensity, narrow-minded prejudice, clear and unwavering judgment

8-9. In the first paragraph, the speaker characterized the students primarily by describing their A. Attitudes B. Possessions C. Physical appearance D. Interactions with each other E. Interactions with their parents

10. The characters are described in terms of which of the following aspects of the lives? I. Social II. Physical III. Financial IV. Intellectual.

11. The characterization of ___ in lines 21-25 is marked by A. Hints of changes that will occur later B. Repetition of descriptive terms C. Implication about the nature of their lives D. An emphasis on the alienation from the scene in the passage E. A stress on the conflicts between ___ and ___.

12. In the passage, ___ exhibits which of the following character traits? (See "CHARACTER TRAIT CHOICES" above)

ORGANIZATION: (2-3 out of 55)

1. Which of the following pairs of phrases most probably refers to the same moment in the sequence of events in the poem?

2. The speaker makes a categorical assertion at all of the following places in the poem EXCEPT

3. Which of the following best describes the order which objects are presented in paragraph one? A. Old to new B. Masculine to feminine C. Large to small D. Familiar to exotic E. Personal to impersonal

4. The words "invariably" (line 23 and "as always" (line 26) contribute which of the following to the development of the passage? I. They characterize the speaker as an experienced observer II. They introduce a sense of continuity relevant to the conclusion of the paragraph III. They provide an indirect comment on the description of the first paragraph.

5. Which of the following best describes the organization of the passage? A. Specific descriptions leading

to a generalization B. Illustration of an abstract idea
by extended definition C. Application of a theory to a
particular situation D. Amassment of imagery to convey a sense of chaos E. Narration of a series of events
leading to a conflict.
6. Which of the following indicates the major shift in
the development of the speaker's exposition? (Use
quoted lines as choices)

STYLE :
A. **Literary Technique:** (4-7 out of 55)
1. The STYLE of the passage as a whole can be best
described as humorless and pedantic, effusive and
subjective, descriptive and metaphorical, terse and epigrammatic, witty and analytical
2. The image of "..." suggests all of the following
EXCEPT the A. Energy generated by ___ B. Power
of God in the Heavens C. Swaying of ___ to the music D. Cohesiveness and unity of the people
E. Despair of those who are bound to earth.
3. The use of the word "..." is an example of which of
the following? Some choices may include:
exaggerated description, ironic reference, euphemism,
allusion, metaphysical conceit, Biblical allusion, Understatement, Oxymoron, self-parody
4. Which of the following lines contain an example
of personification?
5. The dominant techniques in the first paragraph is
the use of hyperbole, puns, lists, euphemisms, abstraction
6. In the second paragraph, the author develops a
contrast between
7. In lines 15-17, ___ makes use of
8. Lines 6-8 have and implied comparison between
thoughts and ___
9. An example of the literary device apostrophe can
be found in line ___
10. The first sentence of the passage is characterized
by which of the following? A. Conventional metrical patterns B. Understatement and economy
C. Romantic diction and imagery D. Periodic form
and balance E. Sardonic mood and atmosphere.

11. The first sentence of the passage is characterized by all of the following EXCEPT: A. Multiple modifiers B. Parallel structures C. Oppressive atmosphere D. Religious imagery E. Ironic wit.

12. In the passage, the ___ functions as A. A symbol of the ___'s plight B. An image of the charm of the ___ C. A comparison of work with leisure D. An emblem of the ___'s influence E. A metaphor for the ___'s leisure.

13. Which of the following are the most prominent IMAGES in the poem? darkness, light, the cross, fellowship, prayer, rebirth, silence, nature, music, sowing, reaping, animal husbandry, movement, growth

B. Diction: (3 out of 55)

1. In context, the adjective " . . ." is best interpreted as meaning

2. The diction used to describe ___ in lines 9-21 suggests that A. Science is slowly beginning to understand certain mysteries B. The speaker finds some aspects of nature alien to her C. Nature is able to provide a truly magical spectacle D. Nature is governed by a higher power E. The beauty of nature is a source of comfort to the speaker.

3. In line 38, the cause of ___ is described in language most similar to that used by the speaker to describe A. Cats B. Birds C. The whippoorwill D. Moths E. The grandfather.

4. The two quotations in lines 15-17 are seen by the speaker as A. Contradictory B. Comforting C. Absurd D. Trite E. Clever.

5. In line 5, " . . ." are mentioned as A. Subjects who loved ___ in former times B. Part of the rabble who oppose legitimate authority C. People in a condition analogous to ___'s state D. The common people who form the backbone of the nation E. Criminals who have committed acts similar to ___.

C. Syntax (Sentence Structure) (0-1 out of 55)

1. The style of the passage as a whole can be characterized by A. Simple declarative sentences containing a minimum of descriptive language B. Complex sentence interspersed with short, exclamatory

statements C. Sentences that contain several modifying phrases and subordinate clauses D. Sentences that grow progressively more argumentative as the passage progresses E. Expository sentences at the beginning that give way to interpretive sentences at the end.

D. Effect: (2-3 out of 55)

1. In lines 12-14, the words " . . ." have which of the following effects? A. They retard the tempo of the speaker's prose B. They satirize ___ C. They highlight the distractions that spoil the audiences concentration D. They change, for a moment, the point of view of the speaker.

2. Which of the following best describes the effect produced by the phrase " . . ." A. It signals to the reader that ___ is an unpleasant event B. It emphasizes how vague ___'s memory is C. It establishes the contrast between ___'s past and future D. It emphasizes the pervasiveness of ___ in ___'s memory E. It alerts the reader to ___' naivete.

3. Which of the following best describes the effect produced by the repetition of the words "seeming" and "seemed" throughout the passage? A. It serves to emphasize ___'s particular perspective on (a certain subject) B. It functions as a reminder to the reader that the narrator is only telling a story C. It suggests that ___'s memory of the events are vague and indistinct D. It provides support for the extended allegory developed in the passage E. It highlights the speaker's capacities as an omniscient narrator.

4. The chief effect of the diction in the sentence " . . ." (lines 25-27) is to provide A. A vivid contrast to the description of ___ B. A strong emphasis on the life of grinding hardship introduced in the sentence " . . ." (lines 23-24) C. An ironic commentary on the villagers who do not possess the virtues of "Love, patience, faith, hospitality" D. An elevated romantic atmosphere that enhances the attitude of the speaker E. A sense of despair and defeat that is inflicted on the villagers by a vengeful deity.

E. Tone: (4-6 out of 55)

1. The IRONY in the passage as a whole rest chiefly in the conflict between A. The solemnity of the occasion

and the joy of the worshippers B. ___'s prophetic wrath and his mother's long suffering C. The air of expectancy and the sounds from the street D. ___'s acute observation of (a happening) and his inability to participate in it E. The change that takes place in the characters and their outward appearance.

2. Which of the following descriptions is an example of the narrator's irony?

3. Which of the following terms are meant to be taken ironically?

4. Which of the following is an irony presented in the poem? A. The ___, apparently under control, is a threat to ___ B. The ___, once in awe of ___, has learned to impose her will on it C. The speaker, able to understand the position of ___, can not comprehend that of ___ D. The ___, once a powerful hunter, has now become a prey E. The ___, through her mastery of ___, has gained the ability to control her own thoughts.

5. The tone throughout the poem can best be described as ___ TWO WORD EXAMPLES OF TONE: playful seriousness, ironic grimness, cheerful glee, somber melancholy, irreversible despair

6. In the poem as a whole, the speaker views nature as being essentially ___
ADJECTIVE EXAMPLES OF TONE:
inspiring, comforting, unfathomable, vicious, benign

7. The grandfather's words convey a sense of ___
NOUN EXAMPLES OF TONE:
regret, awe, tragedy, hope, danger, meanspiritedness, vengeance, amusement, cynicism, disinterestedness, detachment, condescension, pity, enthusiasm, hope

8. The predominant tone of the speaker toward ___ is one of

F. **Rhetorical Purpose: (5-6 out of 55)**

1. The passage is primarily concerned with A. ___'s attitude toward ___ B. ___'s theories about ___ C. The impact of ___ on ___ D. ___'s relationship with ___ E. The role of ___ in the future.

2. The depiction of ___'s " ..." and his mother's " ..." serves what specific function in the narrative progress of the passage? A. It diverts the reader's attention from ___'s point of view B. It retards the pace of the

narration prior to the climax C. It provides a specific example of a preceding general description D. It counters earlier references to ___ E. It offers a parallel to the transformation that the main character undergoes in the passage.

3. The attention the speaker pays to the details of sound serve primarily to A. Distract the reader from the disconcerting issues raised in the passage B. Offer the reader a physical sense of ___ C. Construct a metaphor for ___'s relationship to ___ D. Entertain the reader prior to the presentation of more challenging material E. Complement the attention paid to the visual and the tactile.

4. A principal purpose of the word "shadow" (line 12) is to A. Foreshadow the departure of the speaker B. Emphasize the disintegration of the picture C. Serve as a balance for the use of " . . ." D. Compensate for the negative connotation of " . . ." E. Contrast with the meaning of " . . ."

5. In context, the phrases " . . ." (line 29), " . . ." (line 25), and " . . ." (lines 44-45) serve to A. Evoke an otherworldly atmosphere resonant of the Bible B. Situate the passage within a socially conservative framework C. Highlight the bitter, sardonic humor of the passage D. Mask the passage's truly secular emphasis E. Endorse a particular approach to spiritual matters

6. Lines 44-43 have all of the following functions EXCEPT to A. Return to the initial subject of the poem B. Illustrate the influence of childhood experience C. Link the present to the past D. Emphasizes the chaotic quality of natural events E. Evoke a family relationship.

7. The primary rhetorical purpose of the passage is to A. Characterize a group of people B. Defend the value of a certain life-style C. Dramatize the importance of various possessions D. Illustrate the variety of amusements valued by most people E. Condemn ___'s attitudes toward ___.

8. It can be inferred that the rhythm and diction of the concluding lines are intended to reflect A. ___'s philosophy of life B. The speaker's deep-seated

beliefs C. An objective summary of the day's events
D. ___'s views of his/her own importance E. The
outsider's scorn for ___.
9. In the passage, the speaker uses language primarily to A. Consider his plight B. Soothe his conscience C. Justify his wrongdoing D. Assail his
enemies E. Recreate the past.
10. The succession of phrases ". . ." in lines 10-19
serve to emphasize the A. visible and friendly features of the landscape B. sinister and monstrous
effects of the sun and the clouds C. dramatic and
melancholy quality of the mountains D. Contrast
between the depressed traveler and the impressive
setting E. Paradox that the mountains are both remote and oppressively present.
11. The function of the sentences beginning ". . ." is
to A. Provide examples of B. Defend the ___' lack
of C. Contradict the preceding observations about
beauty and knowledge D. Illustrate the ___'s appreciation for ___ E. Enumerate the simple joys of
___.
12. The description ". . ." serves to A. Recall the
necessity of learning and action B. Qualify a previous generalization about ___ C. Emphasize the complete hopelessness of ___ D. Illustrate the self-con-
fidence and optimism of ___ E. Contradict earlier
statements about ___ in the passage.
13. The central rhetorical strategy of the passage is
to A. Allow the reader to form individual judgments
B. Undercutting the speaker's statements with irony
C. Imitating the language of a certain group of people
D. Beginning and ending on a note of uncertainty
E. Contrasting the setting and its inhabitants.

Chapter Four:

Poetry

Literature and Composition AP

Poetry-
Literature
& Composition
Poetry Questions

Students are encouraged by all English AP Instructors to write often. The types of questions that follow are designed to give students practice in brainstorming and encourage exploration and experimentation. As such, these are not graded with the same type of specific content and mechanics checklists used for AP-type essay exams. In fact, I grade these assignments on two criteria: quantity and variety. I award two points per page (up to 15 pages), but they must select from three of the following categories:

1. Chapter Three: Collaborative Writing
2. Chapter Four, Five or Six: Poetry Questions/Prose Questions/or Drama Questions (Whichever is appropriate to the genre they are reading)
3. Chapter Seven: Creative Suggestions
4. Chapter Eight: Writing Prompts

How to Read & Interpret Poetry

Any poem has three basic parts: its vision, the speaker that expresses that vision, and the language the poet uses to create that voice and vision. The AP Literature essay question on poetry will address the vision or voice of the poem in the stem of the question.

    A. The stem of the question will direct you to describe either:

        1. The speaker's attitude, view of self, assumptions or intentional effect(s), or

        2. The poem's meaning.

    B. The second part of the question will also direct you to show how the language is used to create the stem.

Both the prose and poetry passage, two of the three questions on the essay portion of the exam, will ask you to make the connection between the above two things.

Since AP poems are selected because of their complexity, it is good to begin by discussing the deliberate ambiguities in attitude or meaning which allow for multiple interpretations in the first paragraph of your essay. Also, these different interpretations may form the basis for your organization. The best essays seem to always organize the writing based on the stem, rather than the language. The body paragraphs are then introduced with a topic sentence that defines one of your interpretations of the stem, and is developed with a concentration of how the poet manipulates the language to create that stem. However, never force a set organizational model into an assigned poem. Rather, organize the analysis based on the poem and the directives given to you by the question.

Three Close Reading Steps for Analyzing Poetry:

I. DETERMINE THE LITERAL MEANING (DOMINANT IMPRESSION) OF THE POEM:
    A. Situational Context:
        1. Who is the speaker? Speaker (s)
        2. What kind of person is the speaker?
        3. What is the topic spoken about in the situation / setting ?
        4. What is the occasion: Event, Time (hour, season, Century)
        5. What is the location (one or several?- indoors or out, city or country, land or sea, region, country, or hemisphere) ?
        6. What is the Conflict, if any ? Comparison/contrast? Dilemma?
        7. What are the key images / types of sensory experience (sight, sound, etc.) Groupings of images?
        8. What is the central theme or idea of the poem and how is it achieved?
    B. Type of poem:
        1. Descriptive (imagery without a story)
        2. Narrative (the ballad, dramatic monologue, epic)
        3. Lyrical (expressive of emotional states;

songlike)
4. Topical (poetic essays, commentaries, etc.)
C. Purpose - Which of the following purposes does the poem seem to have?

1. To stress ideas offering insight into human nature and situations or into abstract ideas.
2. To tell a story.
3. To express an emotion.
4. To create a mood or atmosphere.
5. To describe a person, scene or thing
6. To amuse.
7. To satirize.

D. Imagery

1. Is the poem free of images? Does direct language dominate the poem?
2. Does the poet primarily use purely descriptive images, those that appeal to the senses?
3. Is the imagery based on association (the psychological process whereby you are led to link two elements)?
4. Do the images fall into patterns related to the meaning? Do these patterns in effect become dominant symbols lifting the reader beyond the literal level?

II. DETERMINE HOW THE POEM ACHIEVES THIS DOMINANT IMPRESSION. WHAT TYPE OF LANGUAGE DOES THE POET USE TO CREATE THE VISION AND THE VOICE DETERMINED IN STEP I?

A. Poetical Devices:

1. Does one symbol, allegorical device, simile, metaphor or personification seem to dominate the poem?
2. Research any allusions made.
3. What imagery is seen by the combination of all the figurative language used?
4. How does the poet's tone (attitude) bring emotional power to the poem?
5. What sounds contribute to the overall effect of the poem?

B. Language, phrasing and diction:

1. What general term would you use to describe the author's choice of words - artificial and stilted, highly ornate, Latinate, archaic, abstract, conversational or colloquial, rhetorical, sentimental, intensely emotional, trite, etc?

2. Which words are particularly well-chosen, why?

3. What repetitions, synonyms, adjectives, etc. are directly related to attitudes and poet's tone?

4. Does the author rely heavily on unusual words? Why?

5. Does he rely heavily on simple colloquial language? Why?

6. What words seem significant - connotative or suggestive of figurative meaning? How are these words related to the context?

7. Does the poet's desire to present musical effects (meter or rhyme) influence his choice of words? If the influence is heavy, is the quality of the poem marred?

8. Does the poet's time or environment have anything to do with the words he uses? Do any of the words have different meanings today?

9. Can you substitute words of your own for some used by the poet? Which are better? Why? Does this experiment help you understand the difference between poetic diction and ordinary diction?

10. What language is literal ? Figurative

   a. Can you paraphrase the poem on a literal level?

   b. Is there any evidence (such as key words, repetition of symbols, images, etc.) which leads you to suspect that the poem must be taken beyond paraphrase?

   c. Does the poet's tendency to compress material create the possibility of multiple interpretations?

       d. Are there deliberate ambiguities which allow for multiple interpretations?

11. Is there any ironic language (opposite of the usual literal meaning); sarcasm; dramatic irony; paradoxical; Serious vs. Comic language?

12. Other aspects of language

       a. Unfamiliar words- look up in dictionary.

       b. Allusions (look up in an encyclopedia).

       c. Foreign words, phrases (look up in an Oxford Dictionary).

       d. Sound patterns (see also meter below); meaning conveyed or reinforced by sound: alliteration or assonance or consonance

C. Verse = meter (repetition of a syllable pattern)

1. Types of verse = iambic, dactylic, trochaic, anapestic

       a. Iambic meter- A metrical foot consisting of one unstressed syllable followed by one stressed syllable.

       b. Dactylic meter - A metrical foot consisting of one accented syllable followed by two unaccented syllables

       c. Trochaic meter- A metrical foot consisting of one stressed syllable followed by one unstressed syllable.

       d. Anapestic meter- A metrical foot consisting of two unaccented syllables followed by one accented syllable.

2. Length of lines- # of stresses, feet in a each line .

       a. monometer- a metrical line containing one foot

       b. dimeter- a metrical line containing two feet

       c. trimeter- a metrical line containing three feet

       d. tetrameter- a metrical line containing four feet

       e. pentameter- a metrical line containing five feet

       f. hexameter- a metrical line containing six feet

       g. heptameter- a metrical line containing seven feet

       h. octometer- a metrical line containing eight feet

3. Regularity vs. variation - Number of metrical lines per stanza

4. Rhyme scheme (pattern):

5. Refrain (line repetitions)

6. Stanza forms-

       a. Couplet- two rhyming lines

       b. Triplet (tercet)- three rhyming lines

       c. Terza rima- three lines, but only the 1st and last lines rhyme

       d. Quatrain- 4 lines with any combination of rhyme schemes

D. Free Verse - Is the pattern irregular enough to be called free verse?

    1. Poetry that has no regular rhyme or rhythm is free verse.

    2. Free verse relies instead on the natural rhythms of ordinary speech.

    3. Poets writing in free verse may use alliteration, internal rhyme, onomatopoeia, or other musical devices to achieve their effects.

    4. Most poets of free verse place great emphasis on imagery.

E. Musical Characteristics - *Rhythm:*

    1. Can you determine a pattern of stress? Does this pattern fit any of the traditional patterns, such as iambic?

    2. Does the pattern vary? If so, are these variations due to carelessness or do they have pur-

pose (in terms of meaning, emotional intensity, etc.)?

3. What functions do pauses perform in the sound pattern?

4. Are there run-on lines? What effect do these have? How are syntax, syllabication, punctuation, and the lack of punctuation related to sound?

5. Does the purpose and/or meaning of the poem or of a given item or passage help you determine how it should be read (tone of voice, pitch, speed of delivery, etc.)

6. If the music is entirely regular or even monotonous, is this quality due to the failure of the poet or to a purpose which is supported by the poem?

F. Musical Characteristics - *Rhyme:*

1. Is there a rhyme scheme? Is it dictated by convention or is it original?

2. What relevance does the rhyme have to the music of the poem? Does it help or impede the sound pattern?

3. Are there irregular rhymes? If so, why? Are they due to chronological changes in the pronunciation of the words or the poet's desire to pun?

4. If there is no rhyme, is the author using a traditional pattern like blank verse, or does he have some other reason to avoid rhyme. Blank verse is written in unrhymed iambic pentameter (each line contain 5 iambs or feet, consisting of an unstressed syllable followed by a stressed syllable). William Shakespeare uses blank verse.

5. Is internal rhyme used? Why?

6. Does rhyme or absence of rhyme contribute anything to your understanding of the poem?

G. Other Musical Characteristics

1. Does the poet use any of the following musical devices: alliteration (repetition of initial consonant sounds); assonance (repetition of

similar vowel sounds followed by different consonant sounds); consonance (repetition of final consonant sounds after different vowel sounds); onomatopoeia (the use of a word whose sound imitates or suggests its meaning); parallelism (the repetition of words, phrases, or sentences that have the same grammatical structure)?

H. Verse Form

1. Ballad- The typical ballad stanza is a quatrain with the rhyme scheme *abcb*. The second and third line have three stressed syllables; the first and third lines have four stressed syllables. Often the meter is primarily iambic.

2. Epic- A long narrative poem, written in grand language, about a larger than life hero who embodies the values of a society. Included are elements of myth, folklore, history, and legend. Homer's *Odyssey* and *Iliad* and Virgil's *Aeneid,* as well as the Anglo-Saxon poem *Beowulf* and Milton's *Paradise Lost* are among the best known epics.

3. Lyric Poetry- that which focuses on emotions and thoughts rather than on telling a story. John Keats's "To Autumn" and Matthew Arnold's "Dover Beach" are two of the most famous lyrical poems.

4. Ottava Rima- an eight-line stanza in iambic pentameter with the rhyme scheme *abababcc*. Lord Byron's *Don Juan* and William Butler Yeat's "Sailing to Byzantium" are two famous examples of this verse form.

5. Pastoral- a type of poem that depicts rural life in idealized terms, or that expresses a nostalgia for a past age of innocence.

6. Sonnet - a 14 line lyric poem. There are three major types:

a. Petrarchan (Italian)- This sonnet is divided into parts: an eight line octave with the rhyme scheme *abbaabba* and a six line sestet with the rhyme

scheme *cdcdcd*. In most Italian son-
nets the octave describes a situation
and the sestet describes a change in
the situation. The change is called the
turn. The turn signals a logical shift
or new beginning. Sometimes the first
part presents a problem, poses a question, or expresses an idea, which the
sestet then resolves, answers or drives
home. Sometimes the problem is intensified in the sestet with new solution given. John Keats's "On First
Looking Into Chapman's Homer" is
an example of an Italian sonnet (See
Practice Test Two- Essay one).
b. Shakespearean or English sonnet-
This form has three four line units
(quatrains), ending with a two line
unit (couplet). The organization of
thought usually corresponds to this
form. The three quatrains usually
express similar ideas or examples, and
the couplet expresses the concluding
message. The most common rhyme
scheme is *abab bcbc cdcd ee*.
c. Spenserian Sonnet- This sonnet,
like the Shakespearean sonnet, is divided into three quatrains and a couplet, but its rhyme scheme links the
quatrains: *abab bcbc cdcd ee*
7. Spenserian Stanza- a nine line stanza with
a rhyme scheme *ababbcbcc*. The first eight lines
are in iambic pentameter, and the ninth line
is in Alexandrine (a line of iambic hexameter).
Several Romantic poets have used this stanza
form.
8. Villanelle- a nineteen line poem divided
into five tercets (three-line stanzas), each with
the rhyme scheme *aba*, and a final quatrain
with the rhyme scheme *abaa*. Line 1 is repeated
entirely to form lines 6, 12, and 18. Line 3 is
repeated as lines 9, 15, and 19. The two lines

used as refrains (line 1 and 3) are paired as
the final couplet. Dylan Thomas's "Do Not
Go Gentle Into the Good Night" is an example
of a modern villanelle.

III. SO WHAT?

This is the part that makes the highest scores. Somehow you
must attach an individual response to your analysis. This
should be done throughout the written analysis, and certainly
make a good strategy for an effective ending.

A. How do the above devices effect the reader?

B. What sort of difference does this poem make in the
lives of the readers?

C. Does it communicate some new experience or some
fresh understanding of the familiar?

D. Does it express something we have experienced
but have no words to describe?

E. Does the poem engage a combination of the senses,
imagination, intellect, and emotion?

Poetry

Chapter Five:

Prose

Literature and Composition AP

Prose-
Literature
& Composition
Novel/Short Story
Questions

Students are encouraged by all English AP Instructors to write often. The types of questions that follow are designed to give students practice in brainstorming and encourage exploration and experimentation. As such, these are not graded with the same type of specific content and mechanics checklists used for AP-type essay exams. In fact, I grade these assignments on two criteria: quantity and variety. I award two points per page (up to 15 pages), but they must select from three of the following categories:

> 1. Chapter Three: Collaborative Writing
> 2. Chapter Four, Five or Six: Poetry Questions/Prose Questions/or Drama Questions (Whichever is appropriate to the genre they are reading)
> 3. Chapter Seven: Creative Suggestions
> 4. Chapter Eight: Writing Prompts

How to Read & Interpret Prose

The AP Literature essay questions on prose will ask you to analyze how the author manipulates the language to create a specific meaning in a passage
> A. The stem of the question will direct you to define either:
>> 1. The author's (or character's) attitude, view of self, assumptions or intentional effect(s), or
>> 2. The passage's meaning.
> B. The second part of the question will also direct you to show how the language is used to create the stem.

Both the prose and poetry passage, two of the three questions on the essay portion of the exam, will ask you to make the connection between the above two things.

Since AP prose passages are selected because of their complexity, it is good to begin by discussing the deliberate ambiguities in attitude or meaning which allow for multiple interpretations in the first paragraph of your essay. Also, these different interpretations may form the basis for your organization. The best essays seem to always organize the writing based on the stem (the author's --or character's --attitude, view of self, assumptions or intentional effect(s), or the passage's meaning.), rather than the language. The body paragraphs are then introduced with a topic sentence that defines one of your interpretations of the stem, and is developed with a concentration of how the poet manipulates the language to create that stem. However, never force a set organizational model into an assigned poem. Rather, organize the analysis based on the poem and the directives given to you by the question.

Three Close Reading Steps
for Analyzing Prose Passages:

I. DETERMINE THE LITERAL TONE, ATTITUDE, POINT OF VIEW OR MEANING OF THE PASSAGE:
 A. Conflict:
   1. Does the story have important external Conflicts? Do the characters struggle against some outside force (another character, society as a whole, or some natural force)?
   2. Does the story have important internal Conflicts? Do the characters struggle within self between opposing needs, opposing desires, or opposing emotions?
 B. Setting (The time, place, environment, and surrounding circumstances)
   1. Does the setting contribute to the story's emotional effect?
   2. Does the setting reveal the story's conflict?
   3. Does the setting reveal characterization?
 C. Tone, Point of view, or attitude
   1. What is the author's tone?
   2. Who is telling the story? What is the point of view?
   3. What is the main character's attitude?

D. Theme:

    1. Does the story communicate some meaningful insight into human nature of life?

    2. Does the theme deal with important aspects of life? Does it present a new idea or an accepted truth?

    3. What subject dealt with helps to understand the generalization the author wants us to make about life? (old age, ambition, love, prejudice, good vs. evil, distorted views of women, mob justice, religion, money, guilt, courage, etc.)

    4. A theme is not the same as the subject of a work, which can usually be stated in a word or two. Theme is the central idea or insight of the work . . . the idea the author wishes to convey about the subject . . . the writer's view of the world or revelation about human nature. While some themes are directly stated most are implied. It is up to the reader to piece together all the clues the writer has provided about the work's total meaning. Almost all good novels and short stories have some editorializing . . . times in which the author steps outside the storyline and directly states the theme. Two of the most important clues to consider, when the theme is implied, are:

        a. how the main character has changed and

        b. how the conflict has been resolved.

II. DETERMINE HOW THE AUTHOR USES THE LANGUAGE TO CREATE THE TONE, POINT OF VIEW OR MEANING:

    A. Plot

        1. Does the story have unity? Do all the basic elements (conflict, characterization, setting, theme, point of view, and stylistic devices) create a logical purpose or effect?

    B. Characterization:

        Do the personages in the tale:

        1. Exhibit a good reason for being there?

    2. Talk as human beings would talk in a given circumstance?

    3. Have a discoverable purpose?

    4. Have a show of relevancy?

Are the personages in the tale:

    1. Interesting ?

    2. Properly described? Does their conduct and conversation fit these descriptions?

    3. Confine themselves to possibilities and let miracles alone?

    4. Elicit empathy from the reader?

Are the characters in the story

    1. part typical,

    2. part universal,

    3. part individual, and

    4. consistent throughout the story.

C. Narration:

    1. What are the advantages / disadvantages of the author's choice of narration?

    2. Is the point of view consistent? If not, does the writer have a good reason for switching the point of view?

D. Some Literary & Stylistic Elements to consider:

    1. Does the writer should keep the reader's interest by having some:

        a. Foreshadowing

        b. Humor

        c. Excitement

        d. Element of originality

        e. Development of mystery and tragedy

    2. Does the writer "say what he wants to say, not merely come near it" (Twain) by:

        a. Using the right word, not its second cousin.

        b. "eschewing surplusage".

        c. Including all necessary details.

        d. Avoiding slovenliness.

    3. How does the author's use of the following stylistic and rhetorical devices contribute to the story's overall tone, point of view, attitude or meaning?

1. Syntax (Sentence Structure)
2. Satire
3. Poetical devices (Figures of Speech)
4. Symbols
5. Imagery

E. Romanticism: Is the writing Romantic because it displays some of the following characteristics?

1. *Romantic literature* is more imaginative than real: Some people or things are not believable.

2. *Romantic literature* usually pictures an ideal world.

3. *Romantic literature* shows a lot of emotions.

4. *Romantic literature* uses a lot of exaggeration or fabrication that has no real substance.

5. *Romantic literature* has a sympathetic interest in "primitive nature".

6. *Romantic literature* has a sympathetic interest in "Medievalism" (the beliefs of the people in European History between 476 A.D.-1450 A.D.

7. *Romantic literature* is barbarous, uncivilized.

8. *Romantic literature* uses a medieval setting, atmosphere, etc. to suggest horror and mystery.

9. *Romantic literature* uses artificially lofty diction and syntax.

10. *Romantic literature* has a great interest in the picturesque aspects of the past.

F. Naturalism: Does the writing have some of the following characteristics of Naturalism?

1. Characters are doomed to lose because of heredity and environment.

2. The two opposing forces are unequal. Heredity and environment are too much against the protagonist so it is a losing battle.

3. Typical topics for stories include:
    a. Poverty
    b. War
    c. The life and death struggle

d. The deceit and irresponsibility between men and women:

e. The law of the jungle:

f. Child abuse:

g. Unrequited love

4. The characters have some sort of intense
pressure which causes some sort of detachment.

5. Naturalistic stories are unrelenting explo-
sions of evil grossly exaggerated.

G. Realism: Is the writing Realistic because it displays some of the following characteristics?

1. The author goes to great lengths to make
the setting historically accurate.

2. The setting is contemporary to the time it
was written.

3. The characters are fully portrayed as part
typical, part universal, part individual, and
therefore plausible (believable).

4. The two opposing forces are equal in the
conflict, making for a suspenseful plot.

5. The conflict is solved in a believable man-
ner.

6. The characters speak as real people speak.

III. SO WHAT?

This is the part that makes the highest scores. Somehow you
must attach an individual response to your analysis. This
should be done throughout the written analysis, and certainly
make a good strategy for an effective ending.

A. Plot:

1. Is the plot believable and natural, or does
it seem contrived? Does it rely too much on
coincidence and chance?

2. Is the ending satisfying or does it seem a
cliche ending?

3. Is the story suspenseful? Is the writer's
purpose simply to entertain with a "thriller,"
or does the plot involve complex issues and

behavior?

4. Does the tale should accomplish something and arrive somewhere?

5. Are all episodes a necessary development of the tale?

B. Conflict:

    1. Is the conflict significant? If it's significant, it can't be easily resolved. If it's significant, the crisis changes the lives of the characters involved.

    2. Are the two opposing forces equal in strength? If the outcome is never in question, the reader loses interest.

C. Setting:

    1. Is the setting believable

D. Characterization:

    1. Are the characters believable?

    2. Are their motivations (the reasons for their actions) clear and believable? Do they behave consistently?

    3. Do any of the characters change or develop during the course of the story?

    4. To what extent does your story concentrate on the hidden characteristic of the characters?

    5. To what extent is this a story of ordinary men and women - living ordinary lives, frittering away their time on petty activities?

    6. To what extent is this a story of individuals of intensity who awaken our sense of the potential of humans."

E. Theme:

    1. Does the theme seem believable?

    2. Does it relate to human life as I know it?

Chapter
Six:

Drama

Literature
and
Composition
AP

Drama -

Literature
& Composition

Students are encouraged by all English AP Instructors to write often. The types of questions that follow are designed to give students practice in brainstorming and encourage exploration and experimentation. As such, these are not graded with the same type of specific content and mechanics checklists used for AP-type essay exams. In fact, I grade these assignments on two criteria: quantity and variety. I award two points per page (up to 15 pages), but they must select from three of the following categories:

1. Chapter Three: Collaborative Writing
2. Chapter Four, Five or Six: Poetry Questions/Prose Questions/or Drama Questions (Whichever is appropriate to the genre they are reading)
3. Chapter Seven: Creative Suggestions
4. Chapter Eight: Writing Prompts

How to Read & Interpret Drama

The AP Literature essay exam addresses drama only in the open or "free choice" question. Here you are asked to show how one specifically listed part of a suitable play or novel functions in the novel or play as a whole. To do this you must:

A. Provide a reasonable explanation of the meaningful of the work selected, and

B. Make apt and specific references to the text which explains how that specifically listed part contributes to the meaning of the work as a whole. To get a high score here, as with the other essays, you must also

C. Attach an individual response that explains the "So What" aspect of the question.

The following questions are designed to help you in this task:

I. PROVIDE A REASONABLE EXPLANATION OF THE
MEANING OF THE WORK:

   A. Plot: Will a brief summary of the plot will make
the meaning clear?

   B. Types of Drama:

      1. Is your play a Comedy?

         a. Is the audience is amused?

         b. Does the action show a movement
from unhappiness to happiness, en-
tertaining rather than distressing the
audience?

         c. Does the play appeal to the intel-
lect?

      2. Is your play a tragedy?

         a. Does a great person comes to an
unhappy or disastrous end, often
through some lapse in judgment of
character flaw?

         b. Does the play appeal to the emo-
tions?

   C. Characterization: In drama, the characters tell the
tale through their dialogue and actions. There must
not be too many people on stage at any one time, for if
the stage is too crowded, the audience may not be able
to follow the action. In Greek Drama, for instance,
each playwright was limited to three speaking actors.
There is an unlimited number of nonspeaking, walk--
on parts. Consider the following important aspects of
characterization:

      1. Antagonist- who is the person (the bad
guy) or a force (such as the weather) that opposes the protagonist?

      2. Archetype- Is there an image, story pat-
tern or character type which occurs frequently
enough in literature to be recognizable?

      3. Does the Protagonist (the good guy) receive
the sympathies of the reader because the
events center around him/her? because the
narrator is sympathetic toward him/her?

      4. Does a character act as a foil (a character
who, through contrast, shows the character-

istics of a major character)?
D. Empathy-
    1. Does the audience identify with the char-
acters to establish the dramatists desired relationships?
    2. Does the audience feel sympathy for the
major characters (we must be emotionally affected by the fate of these characters if the play
is to be successful)?
    3. Is the audience made to feel that the char-
acters have good reasons for doing what they
do?
E. Dialogue: In a play, what is said and how it is said
are next in importance to character
    1. Is the dialogue is accurate?
    2. Through dialogue can we learn what is
going through a character's mind? (A Dramatic Monologue is a long speech used to reveal a character's thoughts)
    3. Is the dialogue believable?
F. Theme- What is the main idea that the writer of
the literary work wants to convey to the reader?
What is the writer's view of the world or revelation
about human nature?
    1. Antithesis- Does the playwright make a
contrast of ideas expressed in a grammatically
balanced statement?
    2. Irony- Is there any contrast or discrepancy
between what is expected and what actually
is?
        a. Verbal Irony- Does a character say
one thing and means the opposite?
        b. Situational Irony- Is what actually
happens the opposite of the expected?
        c. Dramatic Irony- Does the audience
know something important that a
character in the story or play does not
know?
G. Motif- Does a word, character, object, image, metaphor, or idea recur?
H. Effect: Edgar Allan Poe's "Single Effect" Theory:
Even though Poe's single effect theory refers to a short

story, many similar demands exist for drama. In his famous review of Nathaniel Hawthorne's Twice Told Tales (1842), Poe laid down the rules for what has come to be called the "well-made tale."

1. Does the writer try to establish a preconceived "single effect?" Does he create events that will best aid him in establishing that effect? Does every word add to that effect? (The effect desired by watching a tragedy is one of catharsis.)

2. The length of a short story should be "one sitting" - one to two hours. Does this time limit, imposed on all plays, pose any problems for your play?

3. The effect Poe sought to create was terror, passion, or horror. Does your tragedy have the same effects?

II. MAKE APT AND SPECIFIC REFERENCES TO THE TEXT WHICH EXPLAINS HOW THAT SPECIFICALLY LISTED PART CONTRIBUTES TO THE MEANING OF THE WORK AS A WHOLE:

A. Structure: Plot: explain the progression of action by writing a summary of each of the following:

1. **Exposition**: Where and how does the playwright introduce the characters, setting, and the story's major conflict? Is there some interesting element, a narrative hook, that draws the reader into the story?

2. **Complication**: What developments intensify the conflict? Does each event in the plot relate to conflict? Is there any evidence of foreshadowing? All good writing has cleverly written "hints about future events" which help the reader maintain an active interest in the story.

3. **Climax**: Some critics talk of more than one climatic moment. In drama, one such climatic moment is the turning point or crisis. In Shakespeare's plays, this moment usually occurs in the third act. The turning point is the pivotal moment when the hero's fortunes be-

gin to decline or improve. All the action leading up to this turning point is the rising action, and all the action following it is the falling action. What is the high point of the story?
What happens to resolve the conflict, ending
the story? In Shakespeare's plays, the climax
usually occurs in the last act, just before the
final scene.

4. **Falling action:** How are the mysteries or
problems of the plot are unraveled?
5. **Catastrophe** (the ending of a tragedy):
5. **Denouement** (ending of a comedy):

B. Scene: Does the division of an act indicate a
   1. Stage of action?
   2. Shift in place, or
   3. Change in the number of players on stage?

C. Stage Direction: the dramatists written directions
   1. How the scenes are to be set?
   2. How are lines to be spoken?

D. Character Development-
   1. Does the protagonist learn from the tragedy inflicted upon him and become a more
likable person?
   2. Does the plot involve inner/outer conflict
and some kind of decision?
   3. Does the main character choose to perform
or not to perform some morally meaningful
act that will lead to the play's resolution?
   4. Does the action must involve a noble person who because of a "tragic flaw," and makes
a wrong decision which leads to an unhappy
catastrophe?
   5. Does the experience, although disastrous,
deepen the hero's insight into his/her own
nature and destiny?

III. SO WHAT? To get a high score here, as with the other essays, you must also attach an individual response that explains the "So What" aspect of the question.

A. In his *Philosophy of Composition*, published in 1846, Poe established that the aim of the story was to include, not only truth, the satisfaction of the intellect, but also passion, the excitement of the heart. Are these aims accomplished in your play?

B. Does the tragedy have some catharsis? In feeling pity and fear for the tragic hero, are the viewer's own tensions released and temporarily resolved?

C. What sort of difference does this play make in the lives of the audience?

D. Does it communicate some new experience or some fresh understanding of the familiar?

E. Does it express something we have experienced but have no words to describe?

E. Does the play engage a combination of the senses, imagination, intellect, and emotion?

A Doll's House by Henrik Ibsen

An Act is one of the major divisions of a play; it usually marks a stage in the development of the action. In ancient Greek and Roman plays, the action could generally be divided into five stages of dramatic development: exposition, complication, climax, falling action, and catastrophe (the ending of a tragedy) or denouement (ending of a comedy). The actual division of a play into five stages, which came later, was an attempt to formally indicate this basic structure.

Modern playwrights, however, have come to divide their plays according to their own unique structure rather than attempting to follow this rather abstract pattern.

1. Why did Ibsen divide his plays into three acts?
2. Henrik Ibsen is considered the Father of Modern Drama. How is A Doll's House different from any former plays?
4. Characterization- In drama, the characters tell the tale through their dialogue and actions. There must not be too many people on stage at any one time, for if the stage is too crowded, the audience may not be able to follow the action. In Greek Drama, for instance, each playwright was limited to three speaking actors. There is an unlimited number of nonspeaking, walk-on parts. Does this hold true for A Doll's House ?
5. Who / what is the Antagonist- Why?
6. Who is the Protagonist- Why? _
7. An Archetype is an image, story pattern or character type which occurs frequently enough in literature to be recognizable. Name the archetype in this play- Explain
8. Character Development- Tragedy must have some character growth. The protagonist learns from the tragedy inflicted upon him/her and becomes a more likable person. Explain the development seen in our protagonist:
9. Empathy- The audience must be able to identify with the characters to establish the dramatists desired relationships. In a tragedy, for instance, the audience must feel sympathy for the major characters, for we must be emotionally affected by the fate of these characters if the play is to be successful. Explain to what extent this is true in A Doll's House?
10. Does A Doll's House have a Foil?- Explain:
11. Dialogue- is of vital importance to the success of a play. Aristotle wrote that what is said and how it is said are next in

importance to character, and if the dialogue is not accurate, the audience will not be able to follow the dramatist's ideas. Even the finest of writers of fiction are often unable to pen good dramatic dialogue. The quality of the dialogue, then, is the difference between bad and great plays. Quote one line that would be good or bad based on the above definition. Explain:

12. Theme- The main idea that the writer of a literary work conveys to the reader. The theme is the writer's view of the world or revelation about human nature. What is the main theme of *A Doll's House* ?

13. Irony- a contrast or discrepancy between what is expected and what actually is. Situational Irony occurs when what actually happens is the opposite of the expected. Name one example of Situational Irony:

14. Dramatic Irony occurs when the audience knows something important that a character in the story or play does not know. Name one example of Dramatic Irony:

Choose one of the following questions, using Ibsen's *A Doll's House* as evidence to complete the answer.

Either   Question A:

Some novels and plays seem to advocate change in social or political attitudes or traditions. Note briefly the particular attitudes or traditions that Ibsen wants his 19th Century Victorian audience to change? Then explain how this would apply to today's society. Be sure to include the techniques Ibsen uses to influence the audience's views. Avoid plot summary.

OR

Question B:

What would you say to someone to help him or her distinguish tragedy from pathos? Base your advice on *A Doll's House.*

OR

Question C:

Select one to three scenes in *A Doll's House* that you felt were particularly moving. Compare the playwright's presentation of the respective scene(s), in relation to what you would expect the audience response to be.

Aristotle's Criteria for a Good Play

Tragedy- a drama in which the protagonist suffers disaster but in so doing attains heroic stature, can be understood by viewing it in terms of the original Greek concept described by Aristotle:

1. The plot must involve inner / outer conflict and some kind of decision. The main character must choose to perform or not to perform some morally meaningful act that will lead to the play's resolution.

2. The action must involve a noble person, who because of a "tragic flaw," makes a wrong decision which leads to an unhappy catastrophe.

3. The experience, although disastrous, deepens the hero's insight into his/her own nature and destiny.

4. Tragedy should have some catharsis- the desired effect should be a "purgation" of the emotions of pity and fear; that is, in feeling pity and fear for the tragic hero, the viewer's own tensions are released and temporarily resolved.

Summary: The tragic hero whose character is marked by some tragic flaw, which is ultimately responsible for his downfall, moves us to pity, because his misfortune is greater than he deserves, and to fear, because we recognize similar possibilities and consequences in our own fallible selves.

Aristotle's Definition of Tragedy

Aristotle defined tragedy as "an imitation of an action that is serious, complete, and of a certain magnitude; in language embellished with each kind of artful ornament, the several kinds being found in separate parts of the play, in the form of action, not of narration; through pity and fear affecting the proper purgation of these and similar emotions." To understand this definition, we must define each of the separate terms he used.:

Imitation means finding actions that are universal in that they would appeal to a large audience of various types of people and differing time periods.

Action means the decisions that must be made by the main characters and the ramifications that these decisions make.

Magnitude means that the characters and actions must rise above the ordinary. Although Aristotle's characters were either kings, gods, or great military leaders, Arthur Miller successfully challenged this notion in Death of a Salesman with the creation of Willy Loman, an ordinary tragic hero that was common to all of us.

Ornament includes diction and song . The diction (the way people talk) must be elevated. The songs, choral odes, are sung in ritualistic and often complicated manners. Arthur Miller successfully challenged this too, having ordinary conversation as the basis for his play.

Purgation , or to use Aristotle's term, catharsis, means the feeling of being cleansed that an audience should have at the play's end. The tragic hero moves us to pity, because his misfortune is greater than he deserves, and to fear, because we recognize similar possibilities in our own fallible selves.

The term tragedy does not mean a sad play with an unhappy ending. The point of all tragedy is that the protagonist, even though faced against impossible odds that will eventually cause his destruction, can rise against these odds. It is what he does that counts. A tragic hero will rise in courage and strength to display the godlike qualities that lie within each of us.

Thus tragedy is not a depressing genre. It is positive and optimistic in its view of the possibilities of human potential. The tragic hero must be an individual that has greatness and a stature beyond the ordinary. Because of this the audience experiences the catharsis referred to earlier, when he ultimately fails.

The tragic hero also has to have a "tragic flaw", such as overwhelming arrogance or pride, that leads to his downfall. This flaw could also be a poor choice that leads to his demise. The flaw could also be that he is too virtuous to exist in a world of ordinary beings. Regardless, the hero must be fully aware of what has happened to him in the end and must face that realization. He must proclaim his defiance, as Macbeth did in the end, and welcome his adversary.

There are two other terms to consider when discussing Aristotle's tragedy:

Peripeteia (also called peripety) occurs when an action produces the opposite of what was intended or expected. It is a reversal. Thus, Macbeth kills his king, Duncan, to gain happiness through power, put gains misery instead.

Anagnorisis means disclosure, discovery, or recognition. The tragic hero recognizes himself and his place.

Chapter SEVEN:

CREATIVE SUGGESTIONS

Literature and Composition AP

CREATIVE SUGGESTIONS–

Literature & Composition

AP students should be able to have fun too. The types of activities that follow are designed to encourage exploration, experimentation and FUN. As such, these are graded by the students themselves. I award 10 points for every legitimate hour of work completed. I have my students fill out the chart on the following page when they are completed, and then we agree on a grade. They have a free choice of many activities; however, they must be prepared to share their end product with the class in an appropriate way.

One activity that I feel more and more is very important is memorizing. We teach them that words are powerful when arranged by the masters; we try to get them to emulate good writing; why not have them memorize and recite good passages? Furthermore, the open question requires that they make apt and specific references to the work they've selected. Certainly, memorizing material from the longer works of literary merit assigned will help in the free choice essay.

Allowing this type of activity makes it fun for the teacher as well. These students are very gifted, and when given a bit of free rein, will pleasantly surprise you. The suggestions that follow are just that - suggestions. Students should be able to pick freely and modify the suggestions into an original project that best fits their talents.

Creativity for _____

(Name of Author)

Directions: Each student will select one creative project per author. Students will grade themselves. One hour's work = C... Two hour's work = B .... Three hours work = A. One of these must be done for each author, however, if more than three hours are spent on one particular project, points may be banked and the next assignment lessened or waived. To receive a creative grade of a C for the quarter, you need 8 hours total. To receive a creative grade of a B you need 10 hours total. To receive a creative grade of an A you need 12 hours total.

Name your creative project

_____

How many hours did you spend? _____

How many points did you earn? _____ How many points will be banked? _____

Summarize what you did:

Summarize what you learned:

What was you personal reaction to this assignment?

How will this information be useful to you now or in the future:

Jeopardy

Play the following game of Jeopardy or create one of your own:
The following is a description of how the game of jeopardy can be modified to be used as a fun competition for a class.
The Procedure:
A. The class is divided into teams.
B. One team picks an answer from the grid.
C. The moderator reads the answer.
D. The team discusses the answer and the designated speaker of the group
    1. Provides an answer within 20 seconds, or
    2. Declines to answer.
E. The teacher acts as judge. If the answer is correct, the proper points are added. If answer is wrong, the points are subtracted. If the speaker declines to answer, no points are awarded or subtracted. This continues until the entire square is used.
F. In the final jeopardy round, the teacher tells each class what category is going to be used. The class will then wager X number of points. The teacher will read the answer and give them 30 seconds to respond. If the answer is right, they get the points they waged. If the answer is wrong they lose the points... The team with the most number of points at the end is the winner! Use the chart below to guide the game.

History	Poetry	Quotes	Authors	Myths	Isms
10	10	10	10	10	10
20	20	20	20	20	20
30	30	30	30	30	30
40	40	40	40	40	40
50	50	50	50	50	50

History

_____10. The nickname of the people who were led by Oliver Cromwell.

_____20. This man was the first Archbishop of Canterbury.

_____30. These two royal house were involved in the War of the Roses.

_____40. These are two of the three writers who were forerunners of the Romantic movement and lived during the last half of the 18th Century.

_____50. This author wrote through the eyes of his children from 1651 until his death in 1674.

Poetry

_____10. These three men were known as the Cavalier Poets.

_____20. In England's middle ages this title was given to any eminent poet.

_____30. This poet wrote "The Passionate Shepherd to his Love".

_____40. This English poet was known as the poet of the people and the poet of love.

_____50. This verse form contains lines of iambic pentameter without end rhyme.

Quotes

_____10. "In my younger and more vulnerable years, my father gave me some sound advice that I have been turning over in my mind ever since..." is from this character's thoughts.

_____20. "A little learning is a dangerous thing" was written by this essayist.

_____30. "The people say that the two seemed to be removed from human experience; that they had gone through pain and had come out on the other side; that there was almost a magical protection about them" is from this novel.

_____40. "Never fight fair with a stranger, boy. You'll never get out of the jungle that way." is from this literary work.

_____50. "Lawyers, I suppose, were children once" was written by this person .

Authors

_____10. This author wrote The Iliad.

_____20. This author wrote "The Pardoner's Tale."

_____30. This author, who is famous for modern tragedy, wrote *The Crucible*.

_____40. This Algerian author wrote about the rejection of God.

_____50. This author had his own cosmography of the world.

Mythology

_____10. This gift was sent by Epimetheus by his brother Prometheus.

_____20. This person was an admirer of a vain lad who was turned into a flower.

_____30. This daughter of Demeter causes the changing of seasons.

_____40. This man slayed Medusa.

_____50. This musician played his way into the Underworld to bring back his wife.

Isms

_____10. This ism paid tribute to the senses, emotions, and imagination.

_____20. This mid-nineteenth century Danish writer/philosopher was of the Godly of Theistic existentialists.

_____30. This ism believes that man is at the center of things.

_____40. These writers thought of art as communication rather than expression.

_____50. Mark Twain, Charles Dickens, George Eliot, Thomas Hardy, and Joseph Conrad produced works from this literary movement.

ANSWERS to JEOPARDY on page 120

Internet Activities: Locate, print, and read

1. Book reviews of the text assigned.

> A. Try to establish the credentials of the writer of the review. The reviews could be written by other high school students, other published authors, or the actual author.
>
> B. Examine the organization used by these writers? Do they have a clear thesis? Is their evidence specific? What makes the writing clear?

2. Selected passages of the text assigned.

3. Print pictures of characters, scenes, etc. from your text.

4. A brief chronology of an author, poet, or playwright's life and other works written.

5. General criticism of the text.

6. Games created around texts assigned. One student found a game of jeopardy based on *The Great Gatsby*. The categories were IMAGES, TRANSFORMATION, NICK, GATSBY, NATURE OF TIME, FIVE LETTER WORDS, & FINAL JEOPARDY.

7. E-mail addresses: Write to authors of home pages responding to the information they have created.

8. Copy discussion made about a literary work on a "chat line."

9. Journal site: Many writers have their own Journal site.

10. Censorship: Find examples of a controversial work being banned by schools and libraries. For instance, the *San Francisco Chronicle*, May 29, 1885, wrote an article explaining why the Concord Public Library excluded Mark Twain's new book, *The Adventures of Huckleberry Finn*.

Other Creative Suggestions

1. Make a cover for your notes

2. Draw a picture in response to what you read, or make a collage adding words from the text. Although many students are very artistic, very seldom are they given a chance with a reading assignment to express what they have comprehended through drawing.

3. Address letters to the speaker or main character of a work you are rereading.

4. List just the elements of plot as they occur in your epic poem, novel, short story, or play.

5. Find media pictures that seem to represent certain characters, setting, etc. Write a description of the character, setting, etc. beside the picture.

6. Copy quotations you find interesting. MEMORIZE THEM and recite to teacher. You will be expected to make apt and specific references to the text so memorizing could help you score higher on the open question.

7. Make a vocabulary list of words used by the poet, author, playwright. Define the words.

8. Title Chapters, scenes, stanzas, or rename titles.

9. Write a newspaper account of an episode.

10. Write examples of literary devices used by the writer: allusions, symbols, editorializing, imagery (the concrete verbal pictures that appeal to the senses), point of view (method of storytelling), character description, length and rhythm of sentences, figurative language, dialogue (the colloquial phrases of the period), description, thematic statements, nature of time, form and structure, character growth.

11. Make a chart ("coded notes") showing how one basic element is advanced in the novel.
CHAPTER   CHARACTER OF _____

12. Copy well-written descriptions of the setting or of any of the basic elements of fiction.
      A. Write questions that help understand the passage.
      B. Write AP essay questions on attitude, literary elements, effect or meaning.

13. Copy examples of two word descriptions used in the work. For example: unrevealed capacity, breathless intensity, ripe mystery, scarcely withered, ravenously and unscrupulously, squeaked fashionably, safe and proud, etc.

14. Change general words into more descriptive words:
FUN: engaging, stimulating, enjoyable, consuming, pleasurable, consuming, etc. OKAY: mediocre, marginal, acceptable, etc. ANGRY: furious, degrading, ranting, cross, affected, etc. Try WENT, LITTLE, THINK, SAD, BAD, GOOD, EXAMPLE, DESCRIBE, USE, etc.

15. Update: What would the characters be doing now.

16. Make a list of three syllable words used by the writer.

17. List places most often mentioned in your longer work.

18. Write down adjectives used by the writer to describe the main character's attitude: temperamental, curious, imaginative, smart, tempered, sensible, caring, adventurous, unique, well-educated, thoughtful, motherly, crabby, dreary, etc.

19. Write a newspaper obituary for a character in the text.

20. Write a book review of the text you are reading. Include the following topics:
      A. A statement of the general worth of the book. "The popular appeal of ____ lies in its ability to ____."
      B. A discussion of some of the elements that make the book recommended reading OR NOT.

21. Write down your response to the imagery of the work. Begin with: I see. . . I hear . . . I smell . . . I taste . . . I feel

22. Draw a comic strip version of an episode or do this on the computer as a slide show.

23. Make graffiti (drawings and writings normally scratched on walls) or a mural that illustrates concepts in the work read.

24. Describe the effectiveness of the narration. Was the narrator reliable, an effective communicator, unbiased, etc?

25. Find a poem, play, novel, or short story that relates to the one being read. Explain the relationship.

26. Make a drawing of a character as another character sees him/her.

27. Analyze your previous literary analysis papers by writing just the thesis and topic sentences. Change these so that each reveals a different insight on the same subject.

28. Describe a heroic decision made by a character in your novel, play or poem.

29. Discuss the effectiveness of the work's ending.

30. Make any of the following additions to the text read:
> A. Add scenes that would alter the reader/audience's perception of the character.
> B. Make changes that would strengthen a weak character or weaken a strong character.
> C. Change relationships.
> D. Add editorialized comments to a scene to help illustrate thematic content.
> E. Make the characters's attitude more complex and ambiguous.
> F. Rewrite a scene in terms of being more "politically correct."

"Treasure Hunt" by Allissa Kovala

Directions:

1. Divide into 8 groups of 2 or 3 students.
2. Read the first clue in class. Everyone has the same starting clue.
3. Locate the envelop somewhere in the school building with the first sets of clues.
4. Find the sheet with your group number.
5. Read the next clue for your group (each group has the same clues, but in a different order.
6. Locate the next envelop. Write down the order you followed to get back to the English classroom.
7. The first group back wins a small package of gum.

Here are the clues. The answers are provided, but they would obviously be omitted for the competition.

A. Jay Gatsby had one of these in his back yard:
_____ (Pool)

B. " . . . Had nothing to fear but fear itself." I read this quote from *To Kill a Mockingbird* in this class (not English Language and Composition!) ___(US History)

C. Mertyl was killed by a car driven by Daisy. Daisy would have learned in _____ that she should have stopped after she killed Mertyl. (Driver's Ed)

D. Atticus could play the Jew's Harp in this room.
_____ (Band)

E. Scout was dressed as a ham when she was on the _____ (Stage)

F. Walter Cunningham should have gone here to treat his cooties: _____ (Nurse's Office)

G. Huck had a friend named this. _____(Gym)

H. Huck needed a saw to cut a hole in the cabin wall. You'll find one of these in the _____ (Shop)

I. Scout would always talk to Calpurnia here:
_____ (Kitchen - Home Ec "Laker Shake Shoppe")

J. We read the books *To Kill a Mockingbird, The Great Gatsby, The Adventures of Huckleberry Finn,* and *The Scarlet Latter* in this class: _____ (American Masters-AP)

Poetry

1. Think of a common English word that would be an example of each of the type of feet:

     A. Iamb (short / long)-

     B. Trochee (long / short)-

     C. Spondee (long / long)-

     E. Anapest (short / short / long)-

     F. Dactyl (long / short / short)-

     G. Amphibrach (short / long / short)-

     H. Amphimacer (long / short / long)-

2. Scan your own first and last name. Name its meter by stating its type of foot first and the number of feet next.

     A. Name-

     B. Type of foot-

     C. Number of feet-

3. Scan the first and last names of ten other class members. Name their meter by stating their type of foot first and the number of feet next.

     A.
     B.
     C.
     D.
     E.
     F.
     G.
     H.
     I.
     J.

Computer Game
by Birk Larsen and Nate Swanberg

Name of Project: Big Huck

Hours Spent on Project: About 15-20 Hours Each

Points Earned: 120

Points Banked: 0

Summarize What You Did:

Nate and I created a computer game using many applications on the computer. It was molded after a game that we first saw in about 9th grade that had Bill Clinton called "Slick Willie". There is some general information for the game that should be known to help make sense of the game.

1. All of the gray characters moving on the screen are the Statue of Liberty. This is a metaphor for American freedom. Huck must eat all of them (by moving your mouse) to move on to the next of 11 continually cycling levels.

2. Bonus Items include a Ham, a Raft, and a 50 cent Gold Coin. These items are all worth 50 points if Huck eats them. The ham is a symbol for the search of food. The raft floats by to help Huck get his and Jem's freedom. The gold piece is for Huck to buy necessities.

3. You must avoid all of the bad things:
  a. Pap dripping blood and flashing (because of Huck's escape),
  b. The St. Petersburg times (the newspaper from Huck's town),
  c. A Bloody Knife (the one that Huck used to kill the pig),
  d. A Flaming Building (Jim's shed after the farmers busted in),

    e. Hitler's Head (a metaphor for hatred and racism),

    f. The police Badge (he must avoid the law),

    g. The Skull (a symbol for superstition),

    h. Tom Sawyer (so Huck does not get caught),

Summarize What You Learned:

We learned how to better use the computer, how to create metaphors, how to interpret metaphors, and how to have fun on a long assignment.

Reaction To This Assignment: We enjoyed working with the computer and being able to create this game.

How Will This Information Be Useful To You In The Future:

We have a better understanding of personal and general metaphors and symbols. We also explored different programs and learned how to use them better.

ACADEMY AWARDS

I teach a class called American Masters to Advanced Placement students in the fall. One of the goals of the class is to write comparison/contrast papers, selecting two or three of the major longer works of literary merit assigned. To help them find a "common ground" among these works as a starting point for a topic, I have them vote for their choice of the following categories. Discussing the nominations and selecting a winner, provides many examples of common elements.

Superior Category:

1. Best Supporting Actor:

2. Best Supporting Actress:

3. Most Interesting (complex, amusing, most loved) character:

4. Best Author:

Why?

5. Best Story Line (Explain):

6. Best Theme (Name it):

7. Most Dramatic Scene (Name it):

8. The Funniest Line:

9. The Best Title:

10. The Most Mysterious Character:

11. The Best Conflict:

12. The best Couple:

Wretched Category:

1. The Character I most loved to hate:

2. Reject Award (The book wanted most to throw away:

3. The most empty-headed theme:

4. The Worst Character (Least Well-Rounded):

5. The Worst Author:

6. The Worst Story-line:

7. The worst couple:

8. The Worst Title:

9. The "I Wouldn't Send a Postcard from this Setting" Award:

10. The most boring scene:

More Poetry

Directions: Make groups of 5 words or more for each of the following categories: Riming - Alliteration - Assonance - Synonyms - Other? 100 words are needed.

5. Every Time is Rhyme Time

> A. Compose original sentences with internal rhyme. Each sentence must have four words that rhyme. 15 sentences must be completed.
> B. Examples:

>> 1. "The rain in Spain falls mainly in the plain."

>> 2. "Rubble and stubble make double trouble."

6. Create a Poetry Collage - an artistic composition of fragments of materials pasted on a picture surface.

> 1. This collage should contain a partial or complete definition of poetry.

> 2. This collage should contain a poem or parts of poetry to illustrate that definition.

> 3. The poetry must be typed, printed, or in some other neat, legible, readable manner displayed on the college.

> 4. The collage should be larger than regular sized paper unless a particular artistic shape is used.

> 5. Paper suggested would be construction, tag board, etc.

> 6. The collage should be proper for display purposes.

ART OPTIONS:

1. Make a scarecrow image of a character. Make a cross out of two 1X1 boards. Attach to a 2X4 base. Cut a circle out of cardboard. Draw a face on the circle and attach as head. Clothe the crossed boards in baby clothing. Add hair or hat to make more authentic.

2. Make a plywood poster. Cut a thin plywood board down to a 3' X 3' size. Paint background white. Draw and paint colored version of the title of the text being illustrated. Add painted symbols to surround title.

3. Make Leggo constructions that would represent symbols, settings, characters, etc. in your text.

4. Decorate an old three-bladed fan to illustrate relationships. For instance. Place a symbol of a main character in the middle. The decorate each blade with concerns, topic, themes, other characters, etc. that are related to the main character symbolized in the middle of the fan.

5. Construct a setting on a small plywood base. Include buildings, vegetation, roads, etc.

6. Draw a caricature of a character in a text.

7. Make a humorous, condensed version of some of the longer works of fiction you have been assigned to read. Example:
   A. *Moby Dick:* Ahab chases whale. Whale chases Ahab. Whale prevails.
   B. *Romeo & Juliet:* Two teenagers fall in love and then they die.
   C. *Gone with the Wind:* Scarlet's a yuppie. The South falls. Rhett splits.
   D. *A Tale of Two Cities:* Good times. Bad times. The peasants win. Marie loses.
   E. *War and Peace:* A lot of Russians with long names doing complicated things. The Czars lose.

   Anonymous

ANSWERS to JEOPARDY:

History

10. What were the Roundheads?
20. Who was St. Augustine?
30. Who were The House of Lancester and the House of New York?
40. Who were Thomas Gray, Robert Burns, William Blake?
50. Who is Milton?

Poetry

10. Who were Herrick, Lovelace and Suckling?)
20. What is a Poet Laureate?
30. Who was Christopher Marlowe?
40. Who was Robert Burns?
50. What is blank verse?

Quotes

10. Who is Nick Carraway, the narrator of *The Great Gatsby*?
20. Who was Alexander Pope?
30. What is *The Pearl* ?
40. What is *Death of a Salesman*?
50. Who is Charles Lamb?

Authors

10. Who is Homer?
20. Who is Geoffery Chaucer?
30. Who is Arthur Miller?
40. Who is Camus?
50. Who is Milton?

Mythology

10. What is Pandora's box?
20. Who was Echo?
30. Who is Persephone?
40. Who is Perseus?
50. Who is Eurydice?

Isms

10. What is Romanticism?
20. Who was Kierkegaard?
30. What is humanism?
40. What are the Neoclassicists?
50. What are the Realists?

Chapter Eight:

Writing Prompts

Literature and Composition AP

Writing Prompts- Literature & Compositio

AP students need practice writing in three different ways:

A. Extended writing,
B. Free writing, and
C. 40 minute writing.

"Extended writing" is that in which the writer works on a longer piece of writing over an extended period of time. All aspects of the writing process are developed: selection of topic, brainstorming, collecting specific evidence, writing drafts, revising, editing, and finishing the piece. Doing all this over an extended period of time allows the student "rest time" to forget the writing and then revisit it later for fresh perspectives. Doing this over an extended period of time allows for more thoughtful reflection on the topic. Doing this over a period of time allows for better struggles over word choice and syntax that is so important to developing more effective writing.

"Free writing" is shorter, varied types of writing that allows the student to explore and experiment with his/her own writing style. This should be done daily, or at least, frequently. Examples that follow are just suggestions. Students should use these as a starting point, developing their own topics as the occasion arises.

"40 minute writing" is the writing unique to the AP test. Students need to practice this on their own as formal, teacher-assigned tasks. Some of these should be graded using the checklists in chapter two, and some should not.

Extended Writing Assignment One

Write a 700-1,000 word paper throughout the quarter following the directions below:

    A. The method of approach and format of the assignment will be at the discretion of the student. For example, you may choose from any of the following:

        1. Analysis of a key passage

        2. Comparison of two key passages.

        3. Commentary on a key passage or a whole work.

        4. Other?

    B. Each candidate should choose ONE of the following, either 1 or 2.

        1. A detailed appreciation of an aspect on ONE work studied in which you

            a. Demonstrate an understanding of the aspect chosen (e.g. genre, period, theme, type of literary study, and

            b. Indicate evidence of careful reading of the work

    OR

        2. A comparative study of an aspect of two works. You may select from the works listed below or choose two other appropriate works:

Miller's *The Crucible*

Shakespeare's *Hamlet*

T. S. Eliot and his contemporaries

Nathaniel Hawthorne's works

Williams' *A Streetcar Named Desire*

O'Neill's *The Emperor Jones*

Euipedes' *Medea*

Twain's *The Adventures of Huckleberry Finn*

Lee's *To Kill a Mockingbird*

Dostoevsky's *Crime and Punishment*

Fitzgerald's *The Great Gatsby*

Note: The two works should be chosen for similarity of genre, period, theme, type of literary study, and methodology. The assignment should:

        a. Demonstrate an understanding of the aspect chosen

        b. Indicate evidence of careful reading of the TWO texts.

A Second Quarter Long Assignment

Write a 1,000 - 1,500 word paper throughout the quarter following the directions below:

A. The student's study will be based three works of their choice, but approved by the teacher.

B. The student will choose the three works based on a similar aspect or a similar theme.

C. The aspect may reflect the interests of the student and the underlying approach to the works studied.
EXAMPLES:
1. Narrative Technique
2. Characterization
3. Portrayal of society in the literature studied
4. Universal perspective of common human problems
5. Universal perspective of portrayal of the family

D. The piece of work need not, necessarily, be in the form of a formal essay but it must be a developed piece of writing.

E. Content and format guidelines:
INTRODUCTION:
1. The works which have been read
2. The reason for the choice of the aspect
3. The direction the study of the aspect has taken
CORE:
Substantiation of what the candidate set out to do, using specific examples from the three works
CONCLUSION:
The candidates personal evaluation of the study and the conclusions reached

Free Writing

1. Explain the choices that would be included in a rewriting of a further passage imitating the style of your writer.

2. Review a scene in one of the plays you read. Write an interior monologue showing how the scene would change if we heard what a minor character is thinking.

3. Have a character from a text write a diary or journal entry.

4. Show how a passage would change if another writer you've studied would write a scene from the play or story.

5. Have one writer question another on a character in another writer's text.

6. Show some original research which is helpful in understanding the text.

7. Write a paper on the sensations elicited by the writer through his/her use of imagery. Comment on their effectiveness or connection to other details in writing (Cite Page).

8. Write a paper on style by copying passage that strike you as well-written and comment on their effectiveness .

9. Be a reporter and write a newspaper account of a dramatic scene in one of the novels. Remember the journalist's formula: tell who, what, when, where, why. Question two or three witnesses who were present in this scene.

10. Make the story into a movie by writing the script. Pick the scenes that would be best selected and explain why.

11. Compare one of the characters in one of the novels to any other character you have read or seen in a movie, from the viewpoint of helping or hurting someone else's personality or character.

12. Write an editorial on the death of one of the characters in

one of the novels, short stories, plays or poems that you have read, as though you were a reporter who happened to see the incident. You may make it as dramatic as you wish.

13. Write a horoscope reflecting various scenes or themes in any of the books.

14. Write a want ads page reflecting concerns of people in the time period of a particular novel.

15. Write a diary entry reflecting a day in the life of one of the characters in the story.

16. Write a news brief explaining a dramatic scene in the story.

17. Write the script for a "Talk Show" interview with an author and/or some of the fictional characters in his book.

18. WRITE POETRY

40 minute Essay Writing

1. Identify the author's attitude toward what he or she is describing. Explain how this perspective shapes the way the writer presents the material.

2. Write a Literature "Open" Question, selecting ideas from the content of the following or select your own.

> A. Choose a work in which the title has significance and show how the meaning of the title is revealed implicitly through the author's use of such devices as contrast, repetition, and allusion.

> B. Choose a novel or play in which the opening chapter or scene is important in revealing the various themes that are important to the overall work.

> C. Choose a novel or play in which the ending doesn't end, but rather, requires the reader to adjust to some ambiguity or uncertainty. In your essay, discuss the appropriateness or inappropriateness of this particu-

lar type of ending.

D. Choose a novel or play of literary merit written before 1900 and discuss its relevance to today's society.

E. Choose a novel or a play in which a minor character plays a major role in the story, perhaps by affecting the plot in a unique way, or perhaps by critically affecting the role of the major character by acting as a foil or a confidante.

F. Choose a novel or play in which the full presentation of the villain creates some reader sympathy for his plight.

3. Analyze Poetry or Passages writing your own questions to guide you. Use the typical questions in Chapter Two as models for your own questions.

4. Find similar poetry or prose passages. Write a comparison contrast essay in which you discuss their similarities and differences.

5. Write essays on previously given AP exams.

6. Write an essay that compare two different translations of the same novel. Albert Camus' *The Stranger,* for instance.

Chapter
Nine

Glossary of
Terms

Literature
and
Composition
AP

Glossary of Terms

used in the 1970 -- 1996 (AP) Advanced Placement
Examinations in:

Literature & Composition

- **Abstraction**

   A concept or value that can not be seen (love, honor, courage, etc.) which the writer usually tries to illustrate by comparing it metaphorically to a known, concrete object. Sometimes this knowledge is hidden or esoteric because it is only known by or meant for a select few.

- **Allegory**

   A story or description that has a second meaning. This is portrayed by creating characters, setting, and/or events which represent (symbolize) abstract ideas.

- **Alliteration**

   The repetition at close intervals of initial consonant sounds.

- **Allusion**

   References to literary, artistic, scientific, or historical people, places, or things by the author to convey tone, purpose, or effect.

- **Ambiguity**

   The expression of an idea in such a way that more than one meaning is suggested. All AP essay passages have some ambiguity. To get the highest scores, students have to make reference to the multiple meanings seen in the passages.

- **Analogy**

   A comparison of two things usually made by an author to show how something unfamiliar is like something widely known. In an essay, if you are not sure if it is a metaphor or a simile, call it an analogy.

- **Anapest**

   A metrical foot that has two unstressed syllables followed by one stressed syllable.

•**Anecdote**

A brief story used in an essay to illustrate a point.

•**Antagonist**

The force or person working against the protagonist-the villain.

•**Antithesis**

A contrast of ideas expressed in a grammatically balanced statement. "To err is human; to forgive, divine."

•**Antecedent**

The noun for which the pronoun stands.

•**Aphorism**

A brief, sometimes clever saying that expresses a principle, truth or observation about life (see assertion).

•**Apostrophe**

A literary device in which the speaker directly addresses someone dead, someone missing, an abstract quality, or something nonhuman as if he/she/it were present. Example" "Ye knew him well, ye cliffs"

•**Approximate Rhyme**

Using words that have some sound correspondence, but the rhyme is not perfect.

•**Aside**

Private words, spoken by an actor to the audience, that are not meant to be heard by other characters in the play.

•**Assertion**

A categorical statement made by the author, speaker, narrator or character which generalizes an opinion, usually about human nature.

•**Attitude**

The author's state of mind or point of view toward himself/herself or another person, place or thing.

•**Ballad Meter**

A ballad is a fairly short story-poem that has some songlike qualities. A typical ballad stanza is a quatrain with the rhyme scheme abcb. The meter is primarily iambic.

•**Blank Verse**

Poetry written in unrhymed iambic pentameter.

•**Characterization**

The process by which the writer reveals the personalities of the people of the work. This can be done in the following ways:

1. Direct author/poet statement: The author may use such direct diction as "cruel, conservative, deceitful, long-suffering," or "self-absorbed"
2. Motivations: Some examples could include misguided altruisms, self-destructive ambition, self-conscious insecurity, financial considerations, or hypocritical tendencies.
3. Physical Description
4. Dialogue
5. Thoughts and feelings
6. Actions
7. Effect on others, etc.

• **Closed Couplet**

Two consecutive lines of poetry that rhyme and present a completed thought.

• **Comic Relief**

Something said or done that provides a break from the seriousness of the story, poem, or play.

• **Comparison - Contrast**

Showing similarities and/or differences. The AP question usually asks for differences. This also asks for a judgment about the relative merits of the two passages. Which one is more effective?

• **Conceit**

A juxtaposition that makes a surprising connection between two seemingly different things. T. S. Eliot is a modern poet known for his use of conceits.

• **Conclusion**

Usually written to reaffirm or finally state the thesis. Other strategies used in the conclusion include expressing a final thought about a subject, summarizing main points, using a quotation, predicting an outcome, making an evaluation or recommending a course of action.

• **Confessional Poetry**

A modern term used to describe poetry that uses intimate and usually painful, disturbing or sad material from the poet's life. Anne Sexton and Sylvia Plath are two modern Confessional poets.

• **Conflict**

The tension created in the story by the struggle or

outcome of the struggle — one of the narrative devices to address when analyzing the tone of the passage. Look for internal, as well as external conflict.

• **Connotative Language**

Words which have implied meaning, emphasizing the feelings or subjectivity that surrounds the word. Denotative language, emphasizing the literal, dictionary meaning, is used to create an objective tone. Consider these aspects of words when analyzing how diction creates attitude, effect or purpose.

• **Contrast**

A literary technique in which the author examines two opposites (like the energy of youth and the infirmity of age, worldly possessions and democratic idealism, academic success and extracurricular activities, a speaker's sophistication and the student's naivete, or a group's smug views and the speaker's implied disapproval of them) to create an attitude, accomplish a purpose of effect or to make an assertion.

• **Control a wide range of the elements of writing**

In mature writing, mature diction, varied syntax and effective paragraph organization combine to convey a clear and insightful evaluation, analysis, impression, or assertion.

• **Dactyl**

A metrical foot with one stressed syllable followed by two unstressed syllables.

• **Deduction**

Which of the following is a logical deduction from the speaker's assertions?

• **Definition**

One means of organizing writing. For example, an abstract idea may be developed with a number of definitions of the idea.

• **Denotative Language**

Denotative words have literal, dictionary meaning, emphasizing an objective tone. Connotative language has implied meaning, emphasizing the feelings or subjectivity that surrounds the word. Consider these aspects of words when analyzing how diction creates attitude, effect or purpose.

- **Description**

    Using vivid words to paint a picture of what the five senses are experiencing. The purpose of a descriptive essay is to create a **dominant impression** through a manipulation of details.

- **Diction**

    Word choice used by the author to persuade or to convey tone, purpose, or effect.

- **Dialogue**

    Conversation between people.

- **Didactic**

    Type of writing that is preachy or bossy.

- **Dilemma**

    A type of conflict in which both choices have some negative connotations.

- **Dramatic Monologue**

    A poem in which the speaker addresses one or more listeners who remain silent or whose replies are not revealed.

- **Dramatize**

    To act

- **Economy**

    A style of writing characterized by conciseness and brevity.

- **Effect**

    The influence or result of something, using such rhetorical strategies as arguments, assumptions, attitudes, contrast, diction, imagery, pacing, or repetition. This effect could include such results as to intensify the speaker's sense of the ridiculous, reveal the speaker's ___ attitude, emphasize the cynicism of ___, reduce ___ to the level of low comic characters, or to glamorize a character.

- **End-stopped lines**

    Lines of poetry that end with punctuation marks.

- **Epigram**

    Certain lines of poetry could have the effect of an epigrammatic summary.

- **Euphemism**

    Describing something distasteful in a positive way.

•**Euphony**

A choice and arrangement of words that creates a pleasant sound.

•**Exposition**

One of four major forms of writing, in which explanations are set forth. The other three types of discourse are called narrative, descriptive, and persuasive.

•**Extended Figure**

Any metaphor, simile, personification, or apostrophe that is developed through several lines or throughout the poem.

•**Feelings**

One purpose of a poem may be to convey a feeling of curiosity, contentment, remoteness, resignation, or foreboding.

•**Foreshadowing**

A literary technique in which the author gives hints about future events.

•**Figures of Speech**

Imaginative comparisons (similes, metaphors, personification, etc.) used by the author to convey tone, purpose, or effect.

•**Foil**

A character who contrasts another character.

•**Foot**

A unit of meter that contains a measure of syllables. Five of the most typical types are anapest, dactyl, iamb, spondee, and trochee.

•**Form**

An AP essay may ask how the writer uses form to accomplish a purpose or create an attitude or effect. Form is the external pattern of the poem. Different types of form include: continuous from (lines follow each other without formal grouping, breaking only at the end of a unit of meaning), stanzaic form, free verse, fixed form (the ballad, Terza Rima, etc.) and blank verse.

•**Flashback**

One aspect of narrative structure in which the writer goes back in time to reveal past history that is somehow important to the story.

•**Foreshadowing**

Another aspect of narrative structure in which the author maintains interest by giving clues about future happenings.

•**Free Verse**

Poetry that does not conform to a regular pattern of rhyme or rhythm. The words are arranged in lines but have no fixed meter.

•**Grotesque**

An element of Gothic Romanticism in which bizarre, fantastically ugly or absurd elements are somehow important to the overall effect of the poem or story.

•**Heroic Couplet**

Two consecutive lines of poetry that rhyme and are written in iambic pentameter.

•**Hyperbole**

A figure of speech in which the author uses overexaggeration or overstatement to create a certain effect, accomplish a particular purpose or reveal an attitude.

•**Iamb**

A metrical foot that has one unaccented syllable followed by one accented syllable.

•**Imagery**

Diction describing the five senses (visual, tactile, auditory, olfactory, and emotional) used by the author to convey tone, purpose, or effect.

•**Internal Rhyme**

Rhyme that occurs within a line of poetry.

•**Inverted Order**

Reversing the normal subject-verb-complement order seen in a sentence. Poets sometimes change this order to conform to rhyme and rhythm patterns. Prose writers may change this order for emphasis.

•**Irony**

A literary device used by prose writers/dramatists in which the writer implies a discrepancy between what is said and what is meant (verbal irony), between what happens and what is expected to happen (situational irony), or between what a character in a play thinks and what the audience knows to be true (dramatic irony).

•**Juxtaposition**

>Placing two persons, places or things next to each other to create an effect, reveal an attitude, or accomplish a purpose. Such juxtaposition could include a married couple, two types of religions, or such abstract ideas as virtue and youth, innocence and egotism, or wealth and poverty.

•**Litotes**

>See understatement.

•**Lyrical Poetry**

>A poem whose main purpose is to express the personal feelings or thoughts of the speaker rather than to tell a story.

•**Manipulation of Language**

>A skillful handling of diction and syntax, used by the author to convey tone, purpose, or effect.

•**Metaphysical Conceit (see Conceit)**

>So-called because they were used by the Metaphysical Poets of the seventeenth century, this type of conceit is especially startling, complex and ingenious.

•**Metaphor**

>A direct comparison in which an unknown item is understood by directly comparing it to a known item Metaphors can be **directly stated** or **implied**. When it is developed throughout the poem or over several lines, it is called an **extended metaphor.** One that has been used too often is called a **dead metaphor;** and one that compares things that are visually or imaginatively incompatible is called a **mixed metaphor.**

•**Meter**

>A set of stressed and unstressed syllables of a poetic line, carefully counted to conform to a regular pattern. Meter is described by the type of foot used (iambic, trochaic, dactylic, or anapestic) and the number of feet in each line (monometer, dimeter, trimeter, tetrameter, pentameter, hexameter, heptameter, or octometer). **Blank verse** is written in iambic pentameter because each foot has an unstressed syllable followed by a stressed syllable, and each line has 5 of these iambic feet.

- **Narrative Structure or Narrative Techniques**

    Using a chronology of events, plot, conflict, character-ization, setting, and other elements of storytelling to convey tone, purpose, or effect.

- **Narrator**

    The person telling the story. Can be described as a participating observer who is partial to someone, a third person narrator who is aware of the main character's thoughts (central omniscient), a non-par-ticipating narrator who is unaware of the main character's thoughts (third person objective), a first person narrator who refers of himself in the third person, a third person narrator who reveals the thoughts of several characters (Omniscient).

- **Naturalism**

    A nineteenth-century literary movement that carried realism to a negative extreme. In naturalistic stories character outcomes are doomed by heredity and en-vironment.

- **Octave**

    An eight line poem, or the first eight lines of a Petrarchan sonnet.

- **One - side - at - a - time method**

    One of two ways to organize a comparison-contrast essay. In this type of organization the writer would discuss all the points of one passage first, then discuss all the points of the other passage second, showing the differences between the two.

- **Onomatopoeia**

    The use of words that imitate the sound it makes (buzz)

- **Organization**

    Process of arranging evidence to support a thesis. This organizational choice could be chronological, spatial, emphatic, simple to complex, definition, cause and effect, deductive, inductive, comparison/contrast, di-vision and classification, examples, analogy, side-by-side, point-by-point, etc.

- **Oxymoron**

    A figure of speech that combines contradictory terms (cheerfully vindictive, jumbo shrimp, deafening si-lence, the living dead).

- **Pacing** - The rate of movement (tempo) of a story may be slower with exposition or description, faster with dramatic incidence, etc.
- **Paradigm**

    A model, ideal or standard.
- **Parallel Structures**

    A stylistic technique in which items in a series are created with identical grammatical structures.
- **Paradox**

    A statement or situation that appears contradictory but is true. For instance, the mountains in a setting of a poem, may be both remote and oppressively present. Metaphysical and Cavalier poets of the 17th century made great use of paradoxes.
- **Paraphrase**

    To restate the content of the poem in prose.
- **Parody**

    A rewriting of a popularly recognized work to make fun of something. Rewriting *Little Red Riding Hood* in more "politically correct" language would be an example of a parody.
- **Petrarchan or Italian Sonnet**

    A 14 line poem organized in two segments: the octave (the first 8 lines) and a sestet (the last six lines. The rhyme scheme is abba, cdcd, efef, gg. The other type of Sonnet is called an Elizabethan or Shakespearean Sonnet.
- **Personification**

    A figure of speech in which inanimate objects are given human qualities (The fog comes in on little cat feet).
- **Persuasion**

    Writing which appeals to the reader's emotions and value systems, encouraging the reader to adopt an attitude or change a position.
- **Plausibility**

    An element of literary judgment. Is the work Believable? Whether the work is Romantic or Realistic, some element of believability must exist for reader empathy to occur.

- **Point - by - point** - one of two ways to organize a comparison-contrast essay. In this type of organization the writer would discuss one aspect of both passages, showing how this one aspect differs; then do the same for a second and third aspect, intertwining evidence from both passages in each paragraph.

- **Point of View**

  The tone or attitude created by the author's manipulation of language. ALSO SEE NARRATOR.

- **Pun**

  A play upon words based on the multiple meanings of words. Puns are usually used to create humor, but can be a serious element in poetry, as well.

- **Purpose**

  The reason for writing an essay, usually based on the effect the writer wants to have on his/her audience.

- **Quatrain**

  A poem of four lines, or a stanza of four lines within a poem.

- **Realism**

  A literary style developed in the nineteenth century that attempts to portray life accurately, without idealizing or romanticizing it.

- **Refrain**

  A repeated word, phrase, or group of lines in poetry.

- **Relevance**

  A free choice question may ask you to discuss how a work of literary merit written before 1900 relates to today's modern reader.

- **Repetition**

  A device used by the writer to emphasize an important character trait, to reinforce the story's theme, to highlight the speaker's attitude, etc.

- **Resolution**

  The conclusion of the story.

- **Rhetorical Purpose**

  Reason for the speaker's remarks; or define the attitude that the author would like the reader to adopt.

- **Rhetorical Structure**

  Any organizational device used by the author to convey tone, purpose, or effect. Such writing choices may include: establishing a thesis, presenting a description, presenting a contrasting description, describing an expectation, posing a question and answering it, beginning a narrative and embellishing it, etc.

• **Rhetorical Strategy**

Writing choices made by the author to accomplish purpose. These may include such things as allowing the reader to form individual judgments, undercutting the speaker's statements with irony, imitating the language of a certain group of people, beginning and ending on a note of uncertainty, or contrasting the setting and its inhabitants. Rhetorical innovation is a mark of good writer.

• **Rhetorical Shift**

A change in attitude, purpose, or effect seen in a literary work For example, a speaker's mode of expression may change from one of criticism to acceptance, homage to entreaty, rationality to enthusiasm, uncertainty to resolution, or languor to determination. The shift may also be more structural, such as a digression from the main subject of the poem, a change from description to narration, counterargument to establish the speaker's credibility, metaphorical application of an image in the poem, or a simile for the relationship between two characters.

• **Rhetorical Question**

A literary device in which a question is asked that actually requires no answer.

• **Rime Royal**

A Chaucerian Stanza composed of seven lines written in iambic pentameter with a rhyme scheme of ababbcc.

• **Romanticism**

A literary movement that emphasizes intuition, imagination, and emotions over reason. Most romantics are outspoken in their love of nature and contempt for material things. Most romantics are concerned with the ideal rather than the real. An AP essay may ask you to address romantic diction or romantic atmosphere.

•**Satire**

A type of writing which makes fun of human weakness, vice, or folly in order to bring about change. Some ways to satirize include mingling the serious and the trivial indiscriminately, juxtaposing religious and political views, using repetition to exaggerate character weakness, vice, or folly, etc.

•**Selection and Presentation of specific detail**

Facts, circumstances, characteristics, techniques, etc., used by the author to convey tone, purpose, or effect.

•**Sestet**

Six lines of poetry, especially the last six lines of a Petrarchan sonnet.

•**Setting**

The time and location of the story. The setting may be used by the writer to create conflict, atmosphere, mood, or character.

•**Shakespearean Sonnet**

A 14 line poem composed of three quatrains, followed by a rhyming couplet. The rhyme scheme is abab, cdcd, efef, gg.

•**Soliloquy**

A long speech made by a character in a play while he/she is alone on stage.

•**Sound**

An element to consider when analyzing poetry. For instance, how do sound device add to the overall effect of the poem?

•**Spenserian Stanza**

A nine line stanza with the rhyme scheme ababbcbcc. The first eight lines are written in iambic pentameter and the last line is **alexandrine** - iambic hexameter. This form was created by Edmond Spenser and used by such poets as John Keats, Percy Byssche Shelly, Lord Byron, and Robert Burns.

•**Symbol**

A person, place or thing that represents something else . . . for instance, the whippoorwill in the poem could be presented as a symbol of death. . . a cross could be a symbol of the villager's plight, etc.

• **Syntax (Sentence Structure)**

The arrangement of words into sentences, used by the author to convey tone, purpose, or effect. These can be described as simple, compound, or complex; argumentative, expository, interpretive or narrative; declarative, imperative, interrogative, or exclamatory.

• **Terza Rima**

An interlocking, 3 line stanza form with the rhyme scheme aba bcb cdc ded, etc.

• **Theme**

The central idea, usually by the writer of a work. Theme deals with the writer's view of the world which implicitly reveals some insight about human nature. A good way to start to define theme is to determine the subject of the work. Some subjects could include religious skepticism, emotional deprivation, hopeless deprivation, excessive wildness, or excessive wealth. A description of the passage and its general theme may include such statement as: A character analysis of two professional people which emphasizes the elements of idealism and selflessness that motivate them; A narrative treatment of the conflicts inherent in the structure of social classes; etc.

• **Tone** - The attitude created by the author's manipulation of language. AP passages dealing with tone are complex and ambiguous. To achieve highest marks on a tone essay, the writer has to define the tone in a specifically complex way. Some example would include: bitterness tempered with maturity, respect strengthened by distance, servility imparted by discipline, perplexity compounded by resentment, or gratitude made richer by love.

• **Total Meaning**

The entire experience communicated by the poem - the sensuous, emotional, intellectual, and imaginative.

• **Tragedy**

A play in which the protagonist comes to an unhappy end. The main character is usually an honorable person whose downfall is caused by what Aristotle called a **tragic flaw** (an error in judgment or character weakness).

- **Transcendentalism**

  A nineteenth century movement in the Romantic tradition which believes that humans can rise above materialism to a higher happiness through simplicity and communion with nature.

- **Understatement (Litotes)**

  A statement that says less than what it means. These are often used to make an ironic point.

- **Wit**

  A quality of writing that combines cleverness with keen perception, especially in the writer's ability to state things that the reader has thought but not been able to express in words.

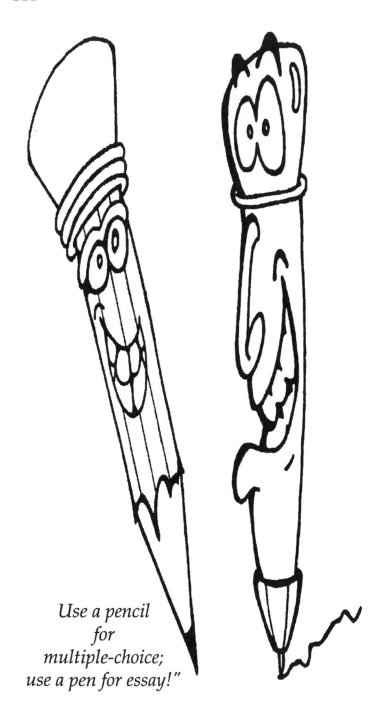

*Use a pencil
for
multiple-choice;
use a pen for essay!"*

Chapter Ten: Practice Tests

Literature and Composition AP

Practice Test 1:

General Instructions

ENGLISH LITERATURE
AND COMPOSITION

Three hours are allotted for this examination: 1 hour for Section I, which consists of multiple-choice questions, and 2 hours for Section II, which consists of essay questions. The multiple-choice questions are printed in this booklet; all essay questions are printed in a separate booklet.

SECTION I

Time — 1 hour

Number of questions - 50

Percent of total grade — 45

This examination contains 50 multiple-choice questions. Therefore, please be careful to fill in only the ovals that are preceded by numbers 1 through 50 on your answer sheet.

General Instructions

DO NOT OPEN THIS TEST BOOKLET UNTIL YOU ARE INSTRUCTED TO DO SO.

INDICATE ALL YOUR ANSWERS TO QUESTIONS IN SECTION I ON THE SEPARATE ANSWER SHEET. No credit will be given for anything written in this examination booklet, but you may use the booklet for notes or scratch work. After you have decided which of the suggested answers is best, COMPLETELY fill in the corresponding oval on the answer sheet. Give only one answer to each question. If you change an answer, be sure that the previous mark is erased completely.

Example: Sample Answer:

Broken Arrow is a   A (B) C D E

(A) state
(B) city
(C) country
(D) continent
(E) village

Many candidates wonder whether or not to guess the answers to questions about which they are not certain. In this section of the examination, as a correction for haphazard guessing, one-fourth of the number of questions you answer incorrectly will be subtracted from the questions you answer correctly. It is improbable, therefore, that mere guessing will improve your score significantly; it may even lower your score, and it does take time. If however you are not sure of the correct answer but have some knowledge of the question and are able to eliminate one or more of the answer choices as wrong, your chance of getting the right answer is improved, and it may be to your advantage to answer such a question.

Use your time effectively, working as rapidly as you can without losing accuracy. Do not spend too much time on questions that are too difficult. Go on to other questions and come back to the difficult ones later if you have time. It is not expected that everyone will be able to answer all the multiple-choice questions.

Note: These directions are copied from the multiple-choice section of *The 1994 Advanced Placement Examination in English Literature and Composition: Free-Response Scoring Guide with Multiple-Choice Section.* Copyright © 1995 by College Entrance Examination Board and Educational Testing Service. All rights reserved.

Practice Test 1:

General Instructions

ENGLISH LITERATURE
AND COMPOSITION

SECTION I -- Time -- 1 hour

Directions: This section consists of selections from literary works and questions on their content, form, and style. After reading each passage or poem, choose the best answer to each question and fill in the corresponding oval on the answer sheet.

Note: Pay particular attention to the requirement of questions that contain the words NOT, LEAST, or EXCEPT.

Questions 1 - 9. Read the following poem written by William Shakespeare carefully before you choose your answers.

Sonnet 18

Shall I compare thee to a summer's day?
Thou art more lovely and more temperate.
Rough winds do shake the darling buds of May,
And summer's lease hath all too short a date.
(50   Sometime too hot the eye of heaven shines,
And often is his gold complexion dimmed;
And every fair from fair sometimes declines,
By chance, or nature's changing course, untrimmed.
But thy external summer shall not fade.
(10)   Nor lose possession of that fair thou ow'st,
Nor shall death brag thou wanderest in his shade
When in eternal lines to time thou growst.
So long as men can breathe or eyes can see,
So long lives this, and this gives life to thee.

_1. Written as an English sonnet, Shakespeare had to follow the formal organization established by all of the following rules for a sonnet EXCEPT: (A) The ideas in the poem must be expressed in 14 lines, no more, no less. (B) Each line has to consist of 10 syllables. (C) The meter has to be iambic pentameter. (D) The verse has to be unrhymed. (E) The sonnet has to have three quatrains and a couplet.

_2. Which of the following characteristics are true of this sonnet? (A) The poem has two four line units, or quatrains. (B) The poem ends with an unrhymed couplet. (C) The rhyme scheme is *abbaabba cdecde.* (D) Three related ideas are expressed in the first two stanzas. (E) The couplet sums up the poet's conclusion.

_3. The logical organization of this sonnet can be best described as which one of the following? (A) Three related ideas are expressed in the first stanza. (B) A question is followed by negative answers. (C) The octave presents a problem that is solved by the sestet. (D) Three problems are posed, with the solution given in the ending couplet. (E) Problems are intensified in each quatrain, and no solution is given.

_4. The beloved "thee" addressed in the sonnet is compared in the first two quatrains to all of the following shortcomings of summer EXCEPT: (A) "Rough winds" (B) "The shortness of "summer's lease" (C) The declining beauty of summer (D) "His gold complexion" (E) "Nature's changing course."

_5. In the context of line 2, the word "temperate" is best understood to mean (A) Pleasant (B) Conservative (C) Abstemious (D) Radical (E) Stormy.

_6. In the context of line 4, the word "lease" is best understood to mean (A) Rental contract (B) Allotted time (C) Let (D) Sublease (E) Sublet.

7. All of the following lines are examples of inversion EXCEPT: (A) "Sometime too hot the eye of heaven shines" (B) "And often is his golden complexion dimmed" (C) "But thy eternal summer shall not fade" (D) "When in eternal lines to time thou growst" (E) ""So long lives this."

_8. The turn, or shift in focus, comes in which line? (A) six (B) seven (C) nine (D) ten (E) twelve.

_9. In the turn, the speaker quits examining summer's faulty day and concentrates on (A) "The darling buds of May" (B) The beloved (C) The heat of Heaven (D) Death (E) The possessions of the poet.

Questions 10 - 14. Read the following poem written by William Shakespeare carefully before you choose your answers.

Sonnet 18

Shall I compare thee to a summer's day?
Thou art more lovely and more temperate.
Rough winds do shake the darling buds of May,
And summer's lease hath all too short a date.
(50   Sometime too hot the eye of heaven shines,
And often is his gold complexion dimmed;
And every fair from fair sometimes declines,
By chance, or nature's changing course, untrimmed.
But thy external summer shall not fade.
(10)   Nor lose possession of that fair thou ow'st,
Nor shall death brag thou wanderest in his shade
When in eternal lines to time thou growst.
So long as men can breathe or eyes can see,
So long lives this, and this gives life to thee.

_10. "Thy external summer shall not fade" can best be described as (A) Playful and inviting (B) Open and sincere (C) Probing and melancholy (D) Ironic and cruel (E) Demanding and sarcastic.

_11. The details of the third quatrain emphasize the woman's (A) Meekness (B) Fastidiousness (C) Assertiveness (D) Wittiness (E) Immortality.

_12. The last two lines of the sonnet serve to emphasize the poet's belief that (A) By being addressed in this poem, all men will see that they are disillusioned by immortality. (B) By addressing the changing course of summer, he realizes there is nothing left to live for. (C) By addressing his loss, he realizes that a persistent and generalized despair eventually comes over all men that breathe. (D) By being addressed in this poem, the beloved has become immortalized. (E) By revealing his love for his beloved, he has exhausted himself.

_13. The poet's attitude toward his beloved can best be described as (A) Enthusiastic and idealistic (B) Reverent and wonder-struck (C) Sarcastic and embittered (D) Resentful and reminiscent (E) Melancholy and reproachful.

_14. Which of the following best describes the sonnet as a whole? (A) An amusing satire on the excesses of summer. (B) A poetic expression of the need for love to give meaning to life. (C) A lyrical celebration of the importance of nature for man. (D) A personal meditation on human courage in the face of destruction. (E) A philosophical and didactic poem about man and nature.

GO ON TO THE NEXT POEM.

Questions 15 - 28. Read the following poem written by "Dover Beach" by Matthew Arnold carefully before you choose your answers.

The sea is calm tonight.
The tide is full, the moon lies fair
Upon the straits; -- on the French coast the light
Gleams and is gone; the cliffs of England stand,
(5) Glimmering and vast, out in the tranquil bay.
Come to the window, sweet is the night air!
Only, from the long line of spray
Where the sea meets the moon-blanched land,
Listen! you hear the grating roar
(10) Of pebbles which the waves draw back, and fling,
At their return, up the high strand,
Begin, and cease, and then again begin,
With tremulous cadence slow, and bring
The eternal note of sadness in.

(15) Sophocles long ago
Heard it on the Aegean, and it brought
Into his mind the turbid ebb and flow
Of human misery; we
Find also in the sound a thought,
Hearing it by this distant northern sea.

The Sea of Faith
Was once, too, at the full, and round earth's shore
Lay like the folds of a bright girdle furled.
But now I only hear
Its melancholy, long, withdrawing roar,
Retreating, to the breath
Of the night-wind, down the vast edges drear
And naked shingles of the world.

Ah, love, let us be true
To one another! for the world, which seems
To lie before us like a land of dreams,
So various, so beautiful, so new,
Hath really neither joy, nor love, nor light,
Nor certitude, nor peace, nor help for pain;
And we are here as on a darkling plain
Swept with confused alarms of struggle and flight,
Where ignorant armies clash at night.

_15. Each of the following words in lines 1-4 define the setting EXCEPT: (A) "sea" (B) "calm" (C) "tide" (D) "moon" (E) "cliffs."

_16. The imagery of beauty and tranquility in lines 4-8 is created by all of the following word choices EXCEPT: (A) "gleams" (B) "gone" (C) "glimmering" (D) "tranquil" (E) "sweet."

_17. Contrasting to the imagery of beauty and tranquility, an undercurrent of something lost or awry, is created by all BUT one of the following: (A) "grating roar" (B) "fling" (C) "begin" (D) "tremulous cadence slow" (E) "eternal note of sadness."

_18. The speaker's tone in lines 1-14 can be described as (A) contented but uncertain (B) remote and disinterested (C) sarcastic and embittered (D) elevated but sympathetic (E) inquisitive but perplexed.

_19. In the context of line 13, "tremulous" is best interpreted to mean (A) blubbery (B) swollen (C) shaky (D) dependable (E) steady.

_20. The reference made to Sophocles, who in *Antigone* likens the disaster that besets the house of Oedipus to the "mounting tide" of the Aegean, helps the reader to see that the speaker's sadness is caused by his awareness of the ravages that history brings to bear on the present. This type of poetical device is known as (A) personification (B) oxymoron (C) allusion (D) simile (E) apostrophe.

_21. In the third stanza, Arnold contemplates the ills of his own time. Faith, which once encompassed humanity, is now only (A) a "sea of faith" (B) "the earth's shore" (C) "a bright girdle unfurled" (D) a "long, withdrawing roar" (D) "the breath of the night wind" (E) "the naked shingles of the world."

Continuing questions on Matthew Arnold's "Dover Beach"

_22. The phrase "naked shingles" (line 28) can be interpreted to mean (A) denizens of evil (B) halls of disrepute (C) sands of time (D) California beaches (E) pebble beaches.

_23. The speaker in this passage is addressing (A) the world (B) his beloved (C) Sophocles (D) the Aegean Sea (E) ignorant armies.

_24. Which of the following statements reveal the speaker's irony? (A) "Ah, love, let us be true/To one another!" (B) "The world" lies "before us like a land of dreams" (C) "The world" is "so various, so beautiful, so new" (D) "The world . . . hath really neither joy, nor love, nor light" (E) "The world" is "swept . . . on a darkling plain."

_25. All of the following words or phrases indicate the predominant ending tone of the speaker EXCEPT: (A) "So various, so beautiful, so new" (B) "a darkling plain" (C) " confused alarms" (D) "struggle and flight" (E) "ignorant armies clash at night."

_26. The tone of the poem changes a third time by the end of the poem to one of outright (A) acceptance (B) indifference (C) hopelessness (D) playfulness (E) sadness.

_27. The speaker's only answer is to (A) trust in God (B) trust in one another (C) be true to your love (D) be true to yourself (E) trust in no one.

_28. All of the following describe Matthew Arnold's poem as a whole EXCEPT: "Dover Beach" is (A) a low-keyed poem compared to the characteristic poems of Romantic and Victorian writers (B) spoken largely in quiet tones (C) spoken in a conversational tone (D) remarkably ambitious in its claim to render a universal condition (E) topical poem written in blank verse.

Questions 29-39. Read the following passages from *The Adventures of Huckleberry Finn* carefully before you choose your answers:

Colonel Grangerford was a gentleman, you see. He was a gentleman all over; and so was his family. He was well-born, as the saying is, and that's worth as much in a man as it is in a horse, so the Widow Douglas said, and nobody ever denied that she was one of the first aristocracy of our town; and pap he always said it, too, though he warn't no more quality than a mudcat himself. Col. Grangerford was very tall and very slim, and had a darkish-paly complexion, not a sign of red in it anywheres; he was clean-shaved every morning all over his thin face, and he had the thinnest lips, and the thinnest kind of nostrils, and a high nose, and heavy eyebrows, and the blackest kind of eyes, sunk so deep that they seemed like they was looking out of caverns at you, as you might say. His forehead was high, and his hair was gray and straight and hung to his shoulders. His hands was long and thin, and every day of his life he put on a clean shirt and a full suit from head to foot made out of linen so white it hurt your eyes to look at it; and on Sundays he wore a blue tail-coat with brass buttons on it. He carried a mahogany cane with a silver head to it. There warn't no frivolishness about him, not a bit, and he warn't ever loud. He was as kind as he could be -- you could feel that, you know, and so you had confidence. Sometimes he smiled and it was good to see; but when he straightened himself up like a liberty-pole, and the lightning began to flicker out from under his eyebrows, you wanted to climb a tree first, and find out what the matter was afterwards. He didn't ever have to tell anybody to mind their manners -- everybody was always good-mannered where he was. Everybody loved to have him around, too; he was sunshine most always -- I mean he made it seem like good weather. When he turned into a cloud-bank it was awful dark for half a minute, and that was enough; there wouldn't nothing go wrong again for a week.

When him and the old lady come down in the morning all the family got up out of their chairs and give them good day, and didn't set down again until they set down....

The old gentleman owned a lot of farms and over a hundred niggers. Sometimes a stack of people would come there, horseback, from ten or fifteen mile around, and stay five or six days, and have such junketings round about and on the river, and dances and picnics in the woods daytimes, and balls at the house nights. These people were mostly kinfolks of the family. The men brought their guns. It was a handsome lot of quality, I tell you.

_29. All but one of the following indicates Huck's attitude here toward aristocracy: (A) The children of aristocratic families all minded their manners. (B) Aristocratic men were all well-born gentlemen. (C) No one of the aristocracy had reddish complexions. (D) Aristocratic people had no more quality than a mudcat. (E) Aristocratic people always entertained stacks of people.

_30. All but one of the following shows how Twain uses contrast to show theme: (A) At the end of this passage he tells us that the men all had guns. (B) He uses the word "darkish-paly" to describe Col. Grangerford (C) He mentions his Pap's lack of quality and reddish complexion. (D) The Grangerfords were obviously different than Huck. (E) The Grangerfords were different than the Widow Douglas.

_31. Which one of the following is an example of the exaggeration Twain uses to characterize the Colonel?

    I. "He had the thinnest lips, and the thinnest kind of nostrils, and a high nose, and heavy eyebrows"

    II. "His hands was long and thin, and every day of his life he put on a clean shirt and a full suit from head to foot made out of linen so white it hurt your eyes to look at it; and

    III. "On Sundays he wore a blue tail-coat with brass buttons on it. He carried a mahogany cane with a silver head to it.

(A) I only (B) I and II (C) I and III (D) III only (E) I, II, and III

_32. Which one of the following is a more negative description of the Colonel's character? (A) "He was as kind as he could be -- you could feel that, you know, and so you had confidence." (B) "Sometimes he smiled and it was good to see" (C) "When he straightened himself up like a liberty-pole, and the lightning began to flicker out from under his eyebrows, you wanted to climb a tree first, and find out what the matter was afterwards." (D) "He didn't ever have to tell anybody to mind their manners -- everybody was always good-mannered where he was." (E) "Everybody loved to have him around, too; he was sunshine most always -- I mean he made it seem like good weather."

_33. All but one of the following shows Twain's use of dialect to characterize Huck: (A) warn't (B) frivolishness (C) clean-shaved (D) good-mannered (E) round about.

_34. All but one of the following topics for theme is alluded to in this passage and developed throughout the novel? (A) Slavery (B) Money (C) Manners (D) Superstition (E) Child Abuse.

_35. Since this passage introduces the feud between the Grangerfords and the Shepherdsons, which of the following statements in this passage is an example of foreshadowing: (A) "The Widow Douglas . . . was one of the aristocracy of our town." (B) "The men brought their guns." (C) Col. Grangerford was very tall and very slim. (D) The old gentleman owned a lot of farms. (E) Sometimes a stack of people would come over there.

_36. The attention that Huck, the narrator, pays to the details that describe the Colonel serves primarily to (A) Distract the reader from the disconcerting issues raised in the passage (B) Offer the reader a physical sense of the Colonel's presence. (C) Counter earlier references to the Colonel's gentlemanly qualities. (D) Entertain the reader prior to presenting more challenging material. (E) Divert the reader's attention from the narrator's point of view.

_37. The point of view in the passage is that of a (A) Naive observer who is partial to the Colonel (B) third person narrator who is aware of the Colonel's thoughts (C) Nonparticipating observer who is unaware of the Colonel's thoughts (D) First-person narrator who chooses to speak of himself in the third-person (E) Third-person narrator who provides insights into the thoughts of several characters.

_38. The style of the passage can best be characterized as (A) Humorless and pedantic (B) Effusive and subjective (C) Descriptive and elevated (D) Terse and epigrammatic (E) Witty and humorous.

_39. The narrator's attitude toward the Colonel can best be described as one of (A) pity (B) Objectivity (C) Sardonic condemnation (D) Emotional judgment (E) Jaded disgust.

Questions 40-50.   Read the following passages from *The Adventures of Huckleberry Finn* carefully before you choose your answers:

It was after sunup now, but we went right on and didn't tie up. The king and the duke turned out by and by looking pretty rusty; but after they jumped overboard and took a swim it chippered them up a good deal. After breakfast the king he took a seat on the corner of the raft, and pulled off his boots and rolled up his britches, and let his legs dangle in the water, so as to be comfortable, and lit his pipe, and went to getting his "Romeo and Juliet" by heart. When he had got it pretty good him and the duke begun to practise it together. The duke had to learn him over and over again how to say every speech; and he made him sigh, and put his hand over his heart, and after a while he said he done it pretty well; "only," he says, "you mustn't bellow out *Romeo!* that way, like a bull - you must say it soft and sick and languishy, so - *R-o-o-meo!* that is the idea; for Juliet's a dear sweet mere child of a girl, you know, and she doesn't bray like a jackass."

Well, next they got out a couple of long swords that the duke made out of long oak laths, and begun to practise the sword fight - the duke called himself Richard III.; and the way they laid on and pranced around the raft was grand to see. But by and by the king tripped and fell overboard, and after that they took a rest, and had a talk about all kinds of adventures they'd had in other times along the river.

After dinner the Duke says:

"Well, Capet, we'll want to make this a first-class show, you know, so I guess we'll add a little more to it . . . . you can do Hamlet's soliloquy.

"Hamlet's which?"

"Hamlet's soliloquy, you know; the most celebrated thing in Shakespeare. Ah, it's sublime, sublime! Always fetches down the house. I haven't got it in the book -- I've only got one volume -- but I reckon I can piece it together from memory. I'll just walk up and down a minute, and see if I can call it back from recollections vaults." . . . .

This is the speech -- I learned it, easy enough . . . .

To be, or not to be; that is the bare bodkin

That makes calamity of so long life;

For who would fardels bear, till Birnam Wood do come to

Dunsinane,

But that the fear of something after death
Murders the innocent sleep,
Great nature's second course,
And makes us rather sling the arrows of outrageous fortune
Than fly to others that we know not of.
There's the respect must give us pause:
Wake Duncan with thy knocking! I would thou couldst;
For who would bear the whips and scorns of time,
The oppressor's wrong, the proud man's contumely,
The law's delay, and the quietus which his pangs might take,
In the dead waste and middle of the night, when churchyards
        yawn
In customary suits of solemn black,
But that the undiscovered country from whose bourn no
        traveler returns,
Breathes forth contagion on the world,
And thus the native hue of resolution, like the poor cat
        i' the addage,
Is sickled o'er with care,
And all the clouds that lowered o'er our housetops,
With his regard their currents turn awry,
And lose the name of action.
'Tis a consummation devoutly to be wished. But soft you,
        fair Ophelia:
Ope not thy ponderous and marble jaws,
But get thee to a nunnery -- go!

_40. The word "rusty" in this passage means all but one of the
following: (A) Clumsy (B) Colorful (C) Unpracticed (D)
Sleepy (E) Blackened.
_41. The word 'bellow' in this passage means all but one of the
following: (A) Shout (B) Whoop (C) Bark (D) Whisper (E)
squawk.
_42. The word "languishy'" in this passage means all but one
of the following: (A) Softly (B) Sickly (C) Listlessly (D)
Hurriedly (E) Sluggishly.
_43. All but one of the following shows Twain's use of dialect
to characterize Huck: (A) He took (B) Chippered them up
(C) Rolled up his britches (D) Had to learn him (E) Got it
pretty good.

_44. This passage implies that the King and the Duke are all but one of the following: (A) lazy (B) English experts (C) con men (D) no-goods (E) bossy.

_45. All but one of the following shows Mark Twain's talent at description: (A) "The King . . . let his legs dangle in the water, so as to be comfortable." (B) " He made him sigh, and put his hand over his heart." (C) " Juliet's a dear sweet mere child of a girl" (D) "They took a rest." (E) "But by and by the king tripped and fell overboard."

_46. In the first line of the Duke's parody of Hamlet's soliloquy, "To be, or not to be" is accurately quoted but confusing because (A) The reader doesn't know the meaning of "bare bodkin" (B) Hamlet's real question is not voiced in the parody (C) The reader needs to know that "fardels" mean "burdens" (D) The words are all inverted (E) "Birnam Wood" and "Dunsinane" are confusing allusions not even used by Shakespeare.

_47. Hamlet's struggle is whether to "suffer the slings and arrows of outrageous fortune, / Or to take arms against a sea of trouble and end them." However, in the Duke's version, the arrows are being slung by (A) Ophelia (B) Hamlet (C) Duncan (D) The Ghost (E) Rosencrantz.

_48. Which one of the following words, correctly quoted by the Duke from Hamlet's soliloquy, make no sense because the words are in a different order: (A) There's the respect "That makes calamity of so long life." (B) "For who would bear the whips and scorns of time" (C) "There's the respect must give us pause" (D) Who would bear "The oppressor's wrong, the proud man's contumely" (E) "Who would fardels bear"

_49. The central rhetorical strategy of Twain's parody of Hamlet's soliloquy is to characterize the duke as (A) an English expert (B) an excellent actor (C) a fraud (D) a friend (E) a screen writer.

_50. The passage suggests that the Duke was (A) Competent and respected by Huck and Jim. (B) Devoted to the interests of Huck and Jim. (C) A servant of the cause of democracy. (D) Using his position for selfish ends. (E) A member of the aristocracy.   END OF SECTION I

        IF YOU FINISH BEFORE TIME IS CALLED, YOU MAY CHECK YOUR WORK ON THIS SECTION.

        DO NOT GO ON TO SECTION II UNTIL YOU ARE TOLD TO DO SO.

Practice Test   1:

"Use A PEN"

ENGLISH
LITERATURE AND COMPOSITION
SECTION II
Time - 2 hours
Number of questions - 3
Percent of total grade - 55

Each question counts as one-third of the total essay score.
Question 1 Essay -- Suggested time. . . . . 40 minutes
Question 2 Essay -- Suggested time. . . . . 40 minutes
Question 3 Essay -- Suggested time. . . . . 40 minutes

Section II of this examination requires answers in essay form. To help you use your time well, the coordinator will announce the time at which each question should be completed. If you finished any question before the time is announced, you may go on to the following question. If you finish the examination in less than the time allotted, you may go back and work on any essay you want.

The quality of the composition will be considered in the scoring of all essay questions. Essays will be judged on their clarity and effectiveness in dealing with the topics. In response to Question 3, select only a work of literary merit that will be appropriate to the question. A general rule of thumb is to use works of the same quality as those you have been reading during your Advanced Placements year(s).

After completing each question, you should check your essay for accuracy and punctuation, spelling, and diction; you Are advised, however, not to attempt many long corrections. Remember that quality is far more important than quantity.

You should write your essays with a pen, preferably in black or dark blue ink. If you must use a pencil, be sure it has a well-sharpened point. Be sure to write CLEARLY and LEGIBLY. Cross out any errors you make.

The questions for Section II are printed in the green insert. Use the green insert to organize your answers and for scratch work, but write your answers in the pink essay booklet. Answer questions in order and number each answer as the question is numbered in the examination. Do not skip lines. Begin each answer on a new page in the pink essay booklet.

Note: These directions are copied from the essay section of *The 1994 AP English Literature and Composition: Free-Response Scoring Guide with Multiple-Choice Section* © Copyright 1995 by College Entrance Examination Board and Educational Testing Service. All rights reserved.

ENGLISH LITERATURE AND COMPOSITION
SECTION II
Total Time -- 2 hours
Question I
(Suggested time — 40 minutes. This question
counts one-third of the total)

Read the following famous soliloquy from Shakespeare's play *Hamlet*, Act 3, scene 1, and its parody from *The Adventures of Huckleberry Finn* that follows. Then write a carefully organized essay analyzing how similar Shakespearean phrases (diction) are manipulated by each writer's different use of syntax to affect meaning and purpose.

Hamlet
          To be, or not to be, that is the question:
          Whether 'tis nobler in the mind to suffer
          The slings and arrows of outrageous fortune,
          Or to take arms against a sea of troubles
(5)   And by opposing end them. To die, to sleep ---
          No more --- and by a sleep to say we end
          The heartache and the thousand natural shocks
          That flesh is heir to. 'Tis a consumation
          Devoutly to be wished. To die, to sleep;
(10)   To sleep, perchance to dream. Ay, there's the rub,
          For in that sleep of death what dreams may come,
          When we have shuffled off this mortal coil,
          Must give us pause. There's the respect
          That makes calamity of so long life.

```
(15)     For who would bear the whips and scorns of time,
         Th' oppressor's wrong, the proud man's contumely,
         The pangs of disprized love, the law's delay,
         The insolence of office, and the spurns
         That patient merit of th' unworthy takes,
(20)     When he himself might his quietus make
         With a bare bodkin? Who would fardels bear,
         To grunt and swear under a weary life,
         But that the dread of something after death,
         The undiscovered country from whose bourn
(25)     No traveler returns, puzzles the will,
         And makes it rather bear those ills we have
         Than fly to others that we know not of?
         Thus conscience does make cowards of us all;
         And thus the native hue of resolution
(30)     Is sickled o'er with the pale cast of thought,
         And enterprises of great pitch and moment
         With this regard their currents turn awry
         And lose the name of action.  --- Soft you now,
         The fair Ophelia, Nymph, in thy orisons
(35)     Be all my sins remembered.
```

3 slings (missiles) **10 rub** (Literally, an obstacle in the game of bowls) **12 shuffled** (sloughed, cast) **12 coil** (turmoil) **13 respect** (consideration) **14 of so long life** (so long-lived, also suggesting that long life itself is a calamity) **15 time** (the world we live in) **16 contumely** (insolent abuse) **17 disprized** (unvalued) **18 office** (officialdom) **18 spurns** insults) **19 of th' unworthy takes** (receives from unworthy persons) **20 quietus** (death) **21 a bare** merely a) **21 bodkin** (dagger) **21 fardels** (burden) **24 bourn** (boundary) **29 native hue** (natural color **30 cast** (tinge, shade of color) **31 pitch** (height - as of a falcon's flight) **31 moment** (importance) **32 regard** (respect, consideration) **32 currents** (courses) **33 Soft you** (i.e. Wait a minute, gently) **34 orisons** (prayers)

from *The Adventures of Huckleberry Finn*
Duke:

        To be, or not to be; that is the bare bodkin
        That makes calamity of so long life;
        For who would fardels bear, till Birnam Wood do come
            to Dunsinane,
        But that the fear of something after death
(5)   Murders the innocent sleep,
        Great nature's second course,
        And makes us rather sling the arrows of outrageous
            fortune
        Than fly to others that we know not of.
        There's the respect must give us pause:
(10)   Wake Duncan with thy knocking! I would thou
            couldst;
        For who would bear the whips and scorns of time,
        The oppressor's wrong, the proud man's contumely,
        The law's delay, and the quietus which his pangs might
            take,
        In the dead waste and middle of the night, when
            churchyards yawn
(15)   In customary suits of solemn black,
        But that the undiscovered country from whose bourn
            no traveler returns,
        Breathes forth contagion on the world,
        And thus the native hue of resolution, like the poor
            cat i' the addage,
        Is sickled o'er with care,
(20)   And all the clouds that lowered o'er our housetops,
        With his regard their currents turn awry,
        And lose the name of action.
        'Tis a consummation devoutly to be wished. But soft
            you, fair Ophelia:
        Ope not thy ponderous and marble jaws,
(25)   But get thee to a nunnery -- go!

Question II
(Suggested time — 40 minutes. This question
counts one-third of the total)

Since the publication of "The Custom House" created such a negative community reaction, Hawthorne made this statement as a preface to his 2nd edition: "As the public disapprobation would weigh very heavily upon him, were he conscious of deserving it, the author begs leave to say that he has carefully read over the introductory pages, with a purpose to alter or expunge whatever might be found amiss, and to make the best reparation in his power for the atrocities of which he has been adjudged guilty. But it appears to him, that the only remarkable features of the sketch are its frank and genuine good humor, and the general accuracy with which he has conveyed his sincere impressions of the characters herein described." And so Hawthorne ends by saying that he has decided to "republish his introductory sketch without the change of a word."

Read the following excerpt from "The Custom House" with the above controversy in mind. Then write a well-organized essay in which you analyze how the author's use of frank humor, selection of details and other resources of language distinguishes his negative toward the community and its members described.

As respects the majority of my corps of veterans, there will be no wrong done, if I characterize them generally as a set of wearisome old souls, who had gathered nothing worth preservation from their varied experience of life. They seemed to have flung away all the golden grain of practical wisdom, which they had enjoyed so many opportunities of harvesting, and most carefully to have stored their memories with the husks. They spoke with far more interest and unction of their morning's breakfast, or yesterday's, today's or tomorrow's dinner, than of the shipwreck of forty or fifty years ago, and all the world's wonders which they had witnessed with their youthful eyes.

The father of the custom house . . . was a certain permanent inspector. He was a man of fourscore years, or thereabouts, and certainly one of the most wonderful specimens of wintergreen that you would be likely to discover in a lifetime's

search. With his florid cheek, his compact figure, smartly ar-
rayed in a bright-buttoned blue coat, his brisk and vigorous
step, and his hale and hearty aspect, altogether he seemed -
not young, indeed - but a kind of new contrivance of Mother
Nature in the shape of a man, whom age and infirmity had no
business to touch. His voice and laugh, which perpetually re-
echoed through the Custom House, had nothing of the tremulous quaver and cackle of an old man's utterance; they came
strutting out of his lungs, like the crow of a cock, or the blast of
a clarion. Looking at him merely as an animal, - and there
was very little else to look at, - he was a most satisfactory
object, from the thorough healthfulness and wholesomeness
of his system, and his capacity, at that extreme age, to enjoy
all, or nearly all, the delights which he had ever aimed at, or
conceived of. The careless security of his life at the Custom
House, on a regular income, and with but slight and infrequent
apprehensions of removal, had no doubt contributed to make
time pass lightly over him. The original and more potent
causes, however, lay in the rare perfection of his animal nature, the moderate proportion of intellect, and the very trifling
admixture of moral and spiritual ingredients; these latter qualities, indeed, being in barely enough measure to keep the old
gentleman from walking on all-fours. . . .

He was, in truth, a rare phenomenon; so perfect, in
one point of view; so shallow, so delusive, so impalpable, such
an absolute nonentity, in every other. My conclusion was that
he had no soul, no heart, no mind; nothing . . . but instincts.

It is time to quit this sketch; on which, however, I
should be glad to dwell at considerably more length, because
of all men whom I had ever known, this individual was the
fittest to be a Custom House officer. Most persons, owing to
causes which I may have space to hint at, suffer moral detri-
ment from this peculiar mode of life. The old Inspector was
incapable of it, and, were he to continue in office ti the end of
time, would be just as good as he was then, and sit down to
dinner with just as good an appetite.

Question 3
(Suggested time - 40 minutes. This questions counts
one-third of the total essay score.)

Good writers use symbols because their evocation of
multiple meanings allow the writer to say more with less. Select a novel, play, or long poem in which settings, characters,
actions, objects, motifs, or names suggest something beyond
its literal meaning. Analyze how the author establishes these
as symbols through the use of such clues as repetition, position, or more than routine emphasis. Then explain how the
symbolic meanings fit comfortably into the context of the story.

Choose a novel, play, or long poem by one of the following authors or another author of comparable merit.

Herman Melville	Margaret Atwood
Fydor Dostoevsky	Jane Austen
Arthur Miller	T. S. Eliot
Henry Fielding	Zora Neal Hurston
Henrik Ibsen	Eudora Welty
Tennessee Williams	Anton Chekov
Charles Dickens	Edith Wharton
William Shakespeare	Edgar Allen Poe
Joseph Conrad	Robert Frost
William Faulkner	Sylvia Plath
Ernest Hemingway	Willa Cather
George Orwell	Sandra Cisneros
John Bunyan	Toni Morrison
Maxine Hong Kingston	Alice Walker
Nathaniel Hawthorne	Virginia Woolf
Albert Camus	Richard Wright

Answers and Explanations

To Practice Test 1:
Section II: Essay

Checklist for
Question 1

from Hamlet's Soliloquy (William Shakespeare) and
the Duke's parody of the same soliloquy (Mark Twain

STEP 1: Subtract one point for each item **not checked** from
the checklist below:

___-___1. The writer demonstrates a perceptive understanding of the meaning and purpose for each soliloquy.

___-___2. The writer analyzes how diction and syntax affect
meaning and purpose in each soliloquy.

___-___3. The writer demonstrates a perceptive understanding of how similar diction is manipulated by each writer's different use of syntax to affect meaning and purpose.

___-___4. The writer makes apt (a minimum of three embedded bits of quotes per paragraph) and specific (detailed and
appropriate) reference to the texts.

___-___5. The writer offers a convincing interpretation of the
purpose for each soliloquy.

___-___6. The writer demonstrates an ability to read perceptively by saying something beyond the easy and obvious to
grasp

___-___7. The writer demonstrates a control over the virtues
of effective communication, including the language unique to
literary criticism.

___-___8. The writer's organization is implicit and original,
yet communicates a clear message.

___-___9. The writer's diction, sentence structure, and grammar aid in communicating a clear message.

MAXIMUM SCORE RESULTS: Grader 1 _____

MAXIMUM SCORE RESULTS: Grader 2 _____

STEP 2: Subtract one point from the results of step 1 for each item **checked** from the rubrics list below. NOTE: To avoid a negative number, you may not have any more checks here than the total on the left.

___-___1. The writer's definition of meaning is oversimplified or vague or omits any discussion of the differing purposes for each soliloquy.

___-___2. The writer discusses the use of diction and syntax with limited purpose or with inappropriate examples.

___-___3. The connection between language and meaning is less clear than those of the top-scoring essays.

___-___4. The writer's use of quotes is awkward, inappropriate, or uninteresting.

___-___5. The writer misreads the meaning or purpose of one or both of the soliloquies.

___-___6. The writer's interpretation is not as persuasive as those of the highest scoring essays.

___-___7. The writer misuses the literary term(s) addressed in the question or omits them partially or entirely.

___-___8. The organization of this essay is less original or implicit than those of the top-scoring essays.

___-___9. The essay reveals consistent weakness in grammar and/or other basic elements of composition.

RESULTS:

Grader 1: _____ - _____ = _____
          Step 1 Score   Step 2 Score

Grader 2: _____ - _____ = _____
          Step 1 Score   Step 2 Score

Grader 1 Score + Grader 2 Score = _____

Above sum / divided by 2 =

Score for essay

Answers and Explanations

To Practice Test 1:
Section II: AP Rubrics

Rubrics for Question 1

from Hamlet's Soliloquy (William Shakespeare) and
the Duke's parody of the same soliloquy (Mark Twain

8-9   These well-written essays demonstrate a clear understanding of how similar Shakespearean diction is manipulated differently by each of the authors to achieve their purpose. The writer presents a clear and relevant thesis — correctly identifying the meaning (or lack of meaning) of each soliloquy — supported by apt and specific evidence from the texts. The organization of these high scoring essays is implicit and clear. Thoroughly convincing, this prose demonstrates the writer's ability to control a wide range of the elements of effective writing, but need not be without flaws.

6-7   These essays also correctly identify the contrasting purposes of each soliloquy, and analyze how the different uses of syntax affect their respective meanings, but the thesis is less specific than the top-scoring essay. Typically they analyze fewer Shakespearean phrases, making the evidence less convincing. The importance of syntax in creating meaning may also be less clear than the top-scoring essay. The organization is less implicit than those of the highest scoring essays. A few lapses in diction, syntax, or use of literary language may be present, but usually the prose of 6 essays convey their writer's ideas clearly.

5   These essays are superficial. They define the meaning of the soliloquies in a typically pedestrian fashion. They deal will the assigned tasks of the question, but they have little to say beyond the easy and obvious to grasp. Their understanding of the importance of syntax in creating meaning may be vague, mechanical, or inadequately supported. While the writing is sufficient to convey the writer's thoughts, these essays are not as well-conceived, organized, or developed as the upper half papers. Often they reveal simplistic thinking and/or immature writing.

3-4   These lower half essays may not answer the entire question. Frequently they misrepresent the purpose of one or both of the soliloquies, analyze syntax and diction with limited purpose or accuracy, or catalogue various phrases in the soliloquies without relating them to purpose and meaning. The prose of 4 essays usually conveys their writers' ideas adequately, but may demonstrate uncertain control over the qualities of college-level composition. They usually contain recurrent stylistic flaws and lack persuasive evidence from the texts.

1-2   These essays demonstrate little or no success in portraying meaning and purpose, and in analyzing how it is conveyed. Some substitute a simpler task, such as paraphrasing the passage or diction and syntax in general. In addition, they are poorly written on several counts and may contain distracting errors in grammar and mechanics. Frequently, they are unacceptably brief. While some attempt may have been made to answer the question, the writer's observations are presented with little clarity, organization, or supporting evidence. Essays that are especially inexact, vacuous, ill-organized, illogically organized and/or mechanically unsound should be scored 1.

Answers and Explanations

To Practice Test 1:
Section II: Results
of Essay 1

from *Hamlet's Soliloquy* (William Shakespeare) and
the Duke's parody of the same soliloquy (Mark Twain)

1-3. The writer demonstrates a perceptive understanding of
the meaning and purpose of each soliloquy, analyzing how
similar diction is manipulated by each writer's different use of
syntax to affect meaning and purpose.

> A. Although both soliloquies use the same diction,
> Shakespeare's is more conventional in purpose, arrang-
> ing the diction in normal syntax to convey Hamlet's
> state of mind.
> B. Twain's parody of Hamlet's soliloquy has a more
> satiric purpose, arranging the diction of Shakespeare
> in nonsensical syntax to make fun of the character of
> the Duke.
> C. With a few obvious changes in syntax,
> Shakespeare's melodious diction becomes meaning-
> less in the Duke's rendition.

4-5. The writer makes apt (a minimum of three embedded bits
of quotes per paragraph) and specific (detailed and appropriate) reference to the text, offering a convincing interpretation
of the purpose and meaning for each soliloquy.

> A. The conning Duke plods through the parody us-
> ing such phrases as "I would thou couldst" and "ope
> not thy ponderous and marble jaws," sounding like
> Shakespeare to the naive audience but appearing idi-
> otic to the educated reader.
> B. Whereas Hamlet ends poetically by asking through
> prayers "be all my sins remembered," the Duke ends
> by quoting a phrase that appears elsewhere in
> Shakespeare's play, "Get thee to a nunnery -- go!"

6. The writer demonstrates an ability to read perceptively by saying something beyond the easy and obvious to grasp.

> A. This comparison reveals that even though words are well-chosen, if they are not arranged in careful order, the result is confusion.
> B. The literal meaning of the reordered diction of the Duke's soliloquy creates humor. Literally, in the first line, the Duke is pondering whether to be, or not to be a knife (bodkin)!
> C. The placement of the words create important, but drastically different significance to each soliloquy.

7, 9. The writer demonstrates a control over the virtues of effective communication, including the language unique to literary criticism, the writer's diction, sentence structure, and grammar. Correct the following:

> A. To be a good writer, one must first establish a creditable basis.
> B. These two masters of their trade use similar phrases to create tremendously different ideas and these ideas are given to the reader.
> C. Even though only Hamlet's soliloquy has meaning, both have purpose, for no one says nothing for no reason.
> D. The Duke's version is totally the opposite than Hamlet's.
> E. The Duke has a version slightly comparing to Hamlet's.
> F. The placement of the words in each soliloquy cause different significance to each one -- Hamlet's words are arranged to tell of his unstable mind; The Duke's words are arranged to tell of his conning character.

Answers and Explanations

To Practice Test 1: Section II: Essay

Checklist for
Question 2

from Nathaniel Hawthorne's "The Custom House"

STEP 1: Subtract one point for each item **not checked** from the checklist below:

___-___1. The writer demonstrates a perceptive understanding of the complexity of Hawthorne's attitude toward the community and its members.

___-___2. The writer analyzes how frank humor, selection of detail, and other resources of the language distinguish Hawthorne's attitude.

___-___3. The thesis clearly shows the connection between Hawthorne's attitude toward the community and its members and the language devices used to convey that attitude.

___-___4. The writer makes apt (a minimum of three embedded bits of quotes per paragraph) and specific (detailed and appropriate) reference to the text.

___-___5. The writer offers a convincing interpretation of the power of Hawthorne's sketch.

___-___6. The writer demonstrates an ability to read perceptively by saying something beyond the easy and obvious to grasp.

___-___7. The writer demonstrates a control over the virtues of effective communication, including the language unique to literary criticism.

___-___8. The writer's organization is implicit and original, yet communicates a clear message.

___-___9. The writer's diction, sentence structure, and grammar aid in communicating a clear message.

MAXIMUM SCORE RESULTS: Grader 1 _____

MAXIMUM SCORE RESULTS: Grader 2 _____

STEP 2: Subtract one point from the results of step 1 for each item **checked** from the rubrics list below. NOTE: To avoid a negative number, you may not have any more checks here than the total on the left.

___-___1. The writer's definition of the attitude is oversimplified or vague or omits any discussion of its irony.

___-___2. The writer discusses the rhetorical and stylistic devices with limited purpose or with inappropriate examples.

___-___3. The connection between the evidence and the author's attitude is less clear than those of the top-scoring essays.

___-___4. The writer's use of quotes is awkward, inappropriate, or uninteresting.

___-___5. The writer misreads the meaning of the passage or simply paraphrases the passage with no reference to the language devices used.

___-___6. The writer's interpretation is not as persuasive as those of the highest scoring essays.

___-___7. The writer misuses the literary term(s) addressed in the question or omits them partially or entirely.

___-___8. The organization of this essay is less original or implicit than those of the top-scoring essays.

___-___9. The essay reveals consistent weakness in grammar and/or other basic elements of composition.

RESULTS:

Grader 1: _____ - _____ = _____
          Step 1 Score   Step 2 Score

Grader 2: _____ - _____ = _____
          Step 1 Score   Step 2 Score

Grader 1 Score + Grader 2 Score = _____

Above sum /
divided by 2 =

Score for essay

Answers and Explanations

To Practice Test 1:
Section II: AP Rubrics

Rubrics for Question 2

from Nathaniel Hawthorne's "The Custom House"

8-9   These well-organized and well-written essays clearly define Hawthorne's complex attitude toward the community and its members. With apt and specific references to the passage, they will analyze how frank humor, selection of detail, and other resources of the language distinguish Hawthorne's attitude. The organization of these high scoring essays is implicit and clear. While not without flaws, these papers will demonstrate an understanding of the text and consistent control over the elements of effective composition. These writers read with perception and express their ideas with clarity and skill.

6-7   These papers also correctly define Hawthorne's complex views of the Custom House members, but they are less incisive, developed, or aptly supported than papers in the highest range. Typically they show how some language or rhetorical devices convey that view, but leave out at least one important element, making the evidence less convincing.   The connection between the evidence and Hawthorne's attitude may also be less clear than the top-scoring essay. The organization is less implicit than those of the highest scoring essays. A few lapses in diction, syntax, or use of literary language may be present, but usually the prose of these essays convey their writer's ideas clearly.

5   Customarily, these essays are superficial. They respond to the assigned topics without important errors, but they do not discuss the irony of Hawthorne's passage. The handling of such elements as frank humor, selection of detail, and other resources of the language may be vague, mechanical, or overly generalized. The writing is adequate to convey the writer's thoughts, but these essays are typically pedestrian, not as well-conceived, organized or developed as upper-half papers. Often they reveal simplistic thinking and/or immature writing.

3-4   These lower half essays may reflect an incomplete understanding of the passage and fail to respond adequately to part or parts of the question. Frequently the discussion of Hawthorne's view is inaccurate or unclear, misguided or undeveloped; these essays may paraphrase rather than analyze. The treatment of frank humor, selection of detail and other resources of the language is likely to be meager and unconvincing. Generally, the writing demonstrates weak control of such elements as diction, organization, syntax, or grammar. These essays typically contain recurrent stylistic flaws and/or misreadings and lack of persuasive evidence from the text.

1-2   These essays compound the weaknesses of the papers in the 3-4 range. They seriously misread the passage or fail to respond to the question. Frequently, they are unacceptably brief. Often poorly written on several counts, they may contain many distracting errors in grammar and mechanics. Although some attempt may have been made to answer the question, the writer's views typically are presented with little clarity, organization, coherence, or supporting evidence.

Answers and Explanations

To Practice Test 1:
Section II: Results
of Essay 2

from Nathaniel Hawthorne's "The Custom House"

1-3. The writer demonstrates a perceptive understanding of the complexity of Hawthorne's attitude toward the community and its members, analyzing how the language is used to distinguish this attitude.

> A. The author's unintentional humor reveals his negative attitude.
>
> B. The author's admiring words, with their negative connotations, create humor for the objective reader -- horror for the living characters described.

4-5. The writer makes apt (a minimum of three embedded bits of quotes per paragraph) and specific (detailed and appropriate) reference to the text, offering a convincing interpretation of Hawthorne's sketch.

> A. The community members "spoke with far more interest and unction" about their daily meals than anything serious, and even seemed to have barely enough moral fiber to keep from "walking on all fours."
>
> B. The "bright-buttoned coat," the "blast of a clarion" in his voice, and the "compact figure" of the representative person contrast the community members' lack of substance.

6. The writer demonstrates an ability to read perceptively by saying something beyond the easy and obvious to grasp.

> A. Hawthorne displays a respect for the physical attributes of the community members, but shows an extremely disparaging attitude toward its moral well being.

8. Do not force the same organization into every essay. Avoid topic sentences that name the device and make a connection to the view, yet say nothing specific.

> A. Selection of detail is used to show Hawthorne's feelings of negativity towards the community.
> B. Hawthorne uses frank humor to show his negative attitude.
> C. The last language device Hawthorne uses to describe his negative attitude is the use of similes

Rather, the writer's organization should be implicit and original, yet communicating a clear message. The highest scores will discuss the language of the passage in a natural way, attaching an individual interpretation to the writing .

> A. Hawthorne's veterans at the Custom House were men with "varied experience of life" who had lost interest in living.
> B.

7, 9. The writer demonstrates a control over the virtues of effective communication, including the language unique to literary criticism, the writer's diction, sentence structure, and grammar. Correct the following:

> A. Everyone has thoughts about the people around them, but if the thoughts are negative, most people keep them to themselves.
> B. In "The Custom House" by Nathaniel Hawthorne, he shows his negative attitude towards the community and its members.
> C. Hawthorne's explanation of the man and his community is sort a visual view of how the man looks.
> D. He describes the features of the inspector, "his hale and hearty aspect," "whom age and infirmity had no business to touch."
> E. The community thought that Hawthorne was comparing the character in such as a way as to make fun of him and the community.

Answers and Explanations

To Practice Test 1:
Section II: Essay

Checklist for
Question 3

Free Reponse on SYMBOLS

STEP 1: Subtract one point for each item **not checked** from the checklist below:

___-___1. The writer selects a suitable novel or play in which settings, characters, actions, objects, motifs, or names, or suggest something beyond its literal meaning.

___-___2. The writer presents a reasonable explanation of the meaning of the work.

___-___3. The writer effectively explains how the author establishes these as symbols through the use of such clues as repetition, position, or more than routine emphasis.

___-___4. The writer effectively explains how the symbolic meanings fit comfortably into the context of the story.

___-___5. The writer makes apt and specific reference to the text.

___-___6. The writer avoids plot summary not relevant to the explanation of the role that symbols play in the evocation of multiple meanings in the work.

___-___7. The writer discusses the literary work with sophistication, insight, and understanding.

___-___8. The writer's displays consistent control over the language unique to the discussion of symbolism.

___-___9. The writer's diction, sentence structure, organization, and grammar aid in communicating a clear message.

MAXIMUM SCORE RESULTS: Grader 1 _____

MAXIMUM SCORE RESULTS: Grader 2 _____

STEP 2: Subtract one point from the results of step 1 for each item **checked** from the rubrics list below. NOTE: To avoid a negative number, you may not have any more checks here than the total on the left.

___-___1. The writer's selection of a symbolically significant play or novel is not as appropriate as those of the higher scoring essays.

___-___2. The writer's explanation of the meaning of the work is less thorough, less specific, or less perceptive than those of the higher scoring essays.

___-___3. The writer's explanation of how the author establishes these as symbols through the use of such clues as repetition, position, or more than routine emphasis may be vague, underdeveloped, or misguided.

___-___4. The writer's explanation of how the symbolic meanings fit comfortably into the context of the story may be less convincing, mechanical, or inadequately related to the work as a whole.

___-___5. The writer's reference to the text lack the specificity of the higher scoring essays.

___-___6. The writer simply paraphrases the meaning of the work with little reference to its symbolic significance.

___-___7. The writer says nothing beyond the easy and obvious to grasp.

___-___8. The writer misuses the literary term(s) necessary to the disscusion of symbolism or omits them partially or entirely.

___-___9. The essay contains distracting errors in grammar and mechanics.   RESULTS:

Grader 1: _____ - _____ = _____
                 Step 1 Score   Step 2 Score

Grader 2: _____ - _____ = _____
                 Step 1 Score   Step 2 Score

Grader 1 Score + Grader 2 Score = _____

Above sum / divided by 2 =

Score for essay

Answers and Explanations

To Practice Test 1:
Section II: AP Rubrics

Rubrics for Question 3

Free Response on SYMBOLISM

8-9   These well-written essays choose appropriate settings, characters, actions, objects, motifs, or names in a novel of play that suggests something beyond its literal meaning. They explain convincingly how these symbols are established by the author to evoke multiple meanings. These papers reflect an understanding of the role of symbolism in fiction and an understanding of the work itself. Superior papers will be specific in their references, cogent in their explications, and free of plot summary not directly relevant to the role that symbolism plays in the work. These essays not not be wiothout flaws, but they demonstrate the writer's ability to discuss a literary work with insight and understanding and to control a wide range of the elements of effective composition.

6-7   These papers also discuss symbolism in an appropriate novel or play. They discuss how symbolism evokes multiple meanings but are less thorough, less perceptive, or less specific than 8-9 papers. They deal with how symbolic meanings fit comfortably into the context of the story, but are less convincing than are the best responses. These essays are wll-written, but with less maturity and control than the top papers. They demonstate the writer's ability to analze a literary work, but they reveal a more limited understanding than do papers in the 8-9 range.

5 Superficiality characterizes these essays. They choose suitable settings, characters, actions, objects, motifs, or names, but their explanation of how these symbols are established by the author to evoke multiple meanings is vague or over-simplified. Their discussion of meaning may be pedestrian, mechanical or inadequately related to the chosen symbolism. Typically, these essays reveal simplistic thinking and/or immature writing. They usually demonstrate inconsistent control over the elements of composition and are not as well-conceived, organized, or developed as the upper-half papers. The writing, however, is sufficient to convey the writer's ideas.

3-4 These lower half essays may choose an acceptable work, but fail to explain how the author establishes symbols to evoke multiple responses. Their analysis of the importance of symbolism is likely to be unpersuasive, perfunctory, underdeveloped, or misguided. The meaning they adduce may be inaccurate or insubstantial and not clearly related to the chosen symbolism. Part of the question may be omitted altogether. The writing may convey the writer's ideas, but it reveals weak control over such elements as diction, syntax, organization, or grammar. Typically, these essays contain significant misinterpretations of the question or the work they discuss; they also may contain little, if any, supporting evidence, and practice paraphrase and plot summary at the expense of analysis.

1-2 These essays compound the weaknesses of the papers in the 3-4 range. They seriously misread the play, novel, or poem, or seriously misinterpret the symbolism they have chosen. Frequently, they are unacceptably brief. Often poorly written on several counts, they may contain many distracting errors in grammar and mechanics. Although some attempt may have been made to answer the question, the writer's views typically are presented with little clarity, organization, coherence, or supporting evidence.

PRACTICE TEST 1 SCORING

NOTE: See separate teacher's guide addendum for answers and explanations for all multiple-choice tests in this book. Add the results of your scores below to determine your AP Grade:

Section I: Multiple-Choice (Total)

_____ - (.25 X _____) = _____ X 1.2273=_____

Number Correct	Number Wrong	Multiple-Choice Score	Weighted Score Section I

Section II: Free-Response

Writing: Essay 1: _____ X 3.0556 = _____

Do not round

Writing: Essay 2: _____ X 3.0556 = _____

Do not round

Writing: Essay 3: _____ X 3.0556 = _____

Do not round

Use CHECKLISTS or RUBRICS on the preceding pages to grade your essays.

Weighted Section II Score

Do not round

Composite Score:

_____ + _____ = _____

Weighted Multiple-Choice Score	Weighted Free-Response Score	**Composite**

Composite Score	AP Grade
150 - 107 (71%)	5
106 - 93 (62%)	4
92 - 74 (49%)	3
73 - 44 (29%)	2
43 - 0	1

Practice Test 2:

General
Instructions

ENGLISH LITERATURE
AND COMPOSITION

Three hours are allotted for this examination: 1 hour for Section I, which consists of multiple-choice questions, and 2 hours for Section II, which consists of essay questions. The multiple-choice questions are printed in this booklet; all essay questions are printed in a separate booklet.

SECTION I
Time — 1 hour
Number of questions - 50
Percent of total grade — 45

This examination contains 50 multiple-choice questions. Therefore, please be careful to fill in only the ovals that are preceded by numbers 1 through 50 on your answer sheet.

General Instructions

DO NOT OPEN THIS TEST BOOKLET UNTIL YOU ARE INSTRUCTED TO DO SO.

INDICATE ALL YOUR ANSWERS TO QUESTIONS IN SECTION I ON THE SEPARATE ANSWER SHEET. No credit will be given for anything written in this examination booklet, but you may use the booklet for notes or scratch work. After you have decided which of the suggested answers is best, COMPLETELY fill in the corresponding oval on the answer sheet. Give only one answer to each question. If you change an answer, be sure that the previous mark is erased completely.

Example: Sample Answer:

   Tulsa is a   A Ⓑ C D E

   (A) state
   (B) city
   (C) country
   (D) continent
   (E) village

Many candidates wonder whether or not to guess the answers to questions about which they are not certain. In this section of the examination, as a correction for haphazard guessing, one-fourth of the number of questions you answer incorrectly will be subtracted from the questions you answer correctly. It is improbable, therefore, that mere guessing will improve your score significantly; it may even lower your score, and it does take time. If however you are not sure of the correct answer but have some knowledge of the question and are able to eliminate one or more of the answer choices as wrong, your chance of getting the right answer is improved, and it may be to your advantage to answer such a question.

Use your time effectively, working as rapidly as you can without losing accuracy. Do not spend too much time on questions that are too difficult. Go on to other questions and come back to the difficult ones later if you have time. It is not expected that everyone will be able to answer all the multiple-choice questions.

Note: These directions are copied from the multiple-choice section of *The 1994 Advanced Placement Examination in English Literature and Composition: Free-Response Scoring Guide with Multiple-Choice Section.* Copyright © 1995 by College Entrance Examination Board and Educational Testing Service. All rights reserved.

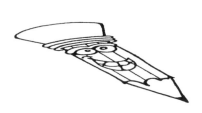

Practice Test 2:

General
Instructions

ENGLISH LITERATURE
AND COMPOSITION
SECTION I -- Time -- 1 hour

Directions: This section consists of selections from literary works and questions on their content, form, and style. After reading each passage or poem, choose the best answer to each question and fill in the corresponding oval on the answer sheet. Note: Pay particular attention to the requirement of questions that contain the words NOT, LEAST, or EXCEPT.

Question 1-16: Read the following poem "Ode on a Grecian Urn" by John Keats carefully before choosing your answers.

1

Thou still unravished bride of quietness,
    Thou foster-child of silence and slow time,
Sylvan historian, who canst thus express
    A flowery tale more sweetly than rhyme:
What leaf-fringed legend haunts about thy shape   (5)
    Of Deities or mortals, or of both
        In Tempe or the dales of Arcady?
What men or gods are these? What maidens loath?
What mad pursuit? What struggle to escape?
        What pipes and timbrels? What wild ecstasy?

2

Heard melodies are sweet, but those unheard   (11)
    Are sweeter; therefore, ye soft pipes, play on;
Not to the sensual ear, but, more endeared,
    Pipe to the spirit ditties of no tone:
Fair youth, beneath the trees, thou canst not leave   (15)
    Thy song, nor ever can those trees be bare;
        Bold lover, never, never canst thou kiss,
Though winning near the goal -- yet, do not grieve;
    She cannot fade, though thou hast not thy bliss,
        Forever wilt thou love, and she be fair!   (20)

3

Ah, happy, happy boughs! that cannot shed
  Your leaves, nor ever bid the spring adieu;
And, happy melodist, unwearied,
  For ever piping songs, for ever new;
More happy love! More happy, happy love!   (25)
   Forever warm and still to be enjoyed,
    Forever painting, and forever young;
All breathing human passion far above,
  That leaves a heart high-sorrowful and cloyed,
    A burning forehead, and a parched tongue.

4

Who are these coming to the sacrifice?   (31)
  To what green altar, O mysterious priest,
Leadest thou that heifer lowing at the skies,
  And all her silken flanks with garlands drest?
What little town by river or sea shore,   (35)
  Or mountain-built with peaceful citadel,
    Is emptied of this folk, this pious morn?
And, little town, thy streets for evermore
  Will silent be; and not a soul to tell
    Why thou art desolate, can e'er return.   (40)

5

O Attic shape! Fair attitude! with brede
  Of marble men and maidens overwrought,
With forest branches and the trodden weed;
  Thou, silent form, dost tease us out of thought
As doth eternity: Cold Pastoral!   (45)
   When old age shall this generation waste,
    Thou shalt remain, in midst of other woe
Than ours, a friend to man, to whom thou sayst,
  "Beauty is truth, truth beauty" -- that is all
    Ye know on earth, and all ye need to know.

_1. The speaker seems to be absorbed in the beginning with the powerful presence of this beautiful urn who "canst thus express a flowery tale more sweetly than our rhyme." This attitude is created by the poet's choice of all of the following EXCEPT: (A) "unravished bride" (B) "foster-child" (C) "sylvan historian" (D) "leaf-fringed legend" (E) "men or gods."

_2. The speaker's excitement is also created by which of the following constructions? (A) One question characterized by periodic form and balance. (B) One question including a series of pleasant, idealized images. (C) One compound-complex sentence. (D) A series of exclamatory statements. (E) A series of short and quickly stated questions.

_3. The speaker is also intrigued that life on the urn is suspended or "frozen" in time. All of the following words or phrases describe this arrested aspect of time EXCEPT: (A) "quietness" (B) "silence and slow time" (C) "who canst thus express" (D) "nor ever can these trees be bare" (E) "never, never canst thou kiss."

_4. All of the following scenes are sculptured on Keats's imaginary urn EXCEPT: (A) Young lovers in flight (B) Young lovers in pursuit (C) A pastoral piper under spring foliage (D) An idyllic marriage with pipes and timbrels (E) The quiet celebration of communal pieties.

_5. In the context of line 3, the word "sylvan" can best be interpreted to mean (A) Rusty (B) Pastoral (C) Crude (D) Vulgar (E) Sophisticated.

_6. In line 7, Keats make use of which of the following? (A) Allusion (B) Oxymoron (C) Understatement (D) Apostrophe (E) Metaphysical conceit.

_7. Which of the following statements best answer why Keats felt that the urn could tell a flowery tale better than his poetry? (A) A "leaf-fringed legend haunts about thy shape" (B) "Heard melodies are sweet, but those unheard/Are sweeter." (C) The urn has "Fair youth, beneath the trees" (D) The woman on the urn is able to stay "forever young." (E) A picture paints a thousand words.

_8. Which of the following words illustrate the poetic license taken by poets to create the wanted rhythm? (A) "loath" (B) "ditties" (C) "e'er" (D) "canst" (E) "brede."

Continuing questions for "Ode on a Grecian Urn"

_9. Keats likes the spirit ditties of no tone because they appeal better to the (A) Imagination (B) Sensual (C) Sense of sight (D) Sense of Touch (E) Sense of sound.

_10. The image of trees who could never lose their leaves is an example of what figure of speech? (A) Simile (B) Paradox (C) Metaphor (D) Analogy (E) Apostrophe.

_11. Which of the following describes the speaker's state at the end of stanza three? (A) He feels mean-spirited and full of vengeance (B) He is amused but cynical. (C) He has become disinterested and detached. (D) He is wearied with excess. (E) He has a new-found enthusiasm and hope.

_12. The third stanza has been criticized as badly written because Keats used happy and forever too many times. However, he did this because he wanted to emulate the effect this urn has on the speaker at this point. Which of the following best describes this effect?

    I. All restraints are abandoned here to live in a forever happy world.
    II. The speaker is so excited he is making no sense.
    III. Keats wishes to emphasize the speaker's state of immortal happiness.

(A) I only (B) II only (C) III only (D) I and II (E) II and III.

_13. A change in attitude can be seen in Keats's use of which phrase? (A) "High-sorrowful and cloyed" (B) "Breathing human passion" (C) "A burning forehead" (D) "A parching tongue" (E) "Cold Pastoral."

_14. In this poem, Keats reflects on all of the following EXCEPT: (A) Religion (B) Love (C) Nature (D) Escape (E) Revenge.

_15. The speaker characterizes the life illustrated on the urn as (A) Immortal and unchanging (B) Happy and forever (C) Mad and insane (D) Contented and smug (E) Pleasant and easygoing.

_16. All of the following are possible interpretations of the ambiguous ending "Beauty is truth -- truth beauty" EXCEPT: (A) Keats preferred the beauty of the urn to the changing reality of life. (B) This statement characterizes the search for beauty that typifies most Romantic writing. (C) This statement is a universal and profound metaphysical proposition. (D) This statement is simply nonsense. (E) This is an overstatement uttered in the course of a dramatic dialogue.

Question 17 - 26. Read the following poem "I Died for Beauty
-- But was Scarce" by Emily Dickinson carefully before choosing your answers.

> I died for Beauty -- but was scarce
> Adjusted in the Tomb
> When one who died for Truth, was lain
> In an adjoining Room --
>
> (5)　He questioned softly "Why I failed?"
> "For Beauty," I replied --
> "And I -- for Truth -- Themself are One --
> We Brethren, are," He said --
>
> 　　And so, as Kinsmen, met at Night --
> (10)　We talked between the Rooms --
> Until the Moss had reached our lips --
> And covered up -- our names --

_17. Lines 1, 3, 5, 7, 9, and 11 are written in iambic (A) Trimeter
(B) tetrameter (C) pentameter (D) hexameter (E) heptameter.

_18. Lines 2, 4, 6, 8, 10, and 12 are written in iambic (A)
Trimeter (B) tetrameter (C) pentameter (D) hexameter (E)
heptameter.

_19. Each quatrain has a rhyme scheme of (A) abca (B) aabb
(C) abab (D) abcb (E) abca.

_20. Slant rhyme occurs in 　　I. Stanza 1
　　　　　　　　　　　　II. Stanza 2
　　　　　　　　　　　　III. Stanza 3
(A) I only (B) II only (C) III only (D) II and III (E) I, II, III.

_21. The two speakers are "Brethern" because they both feel
that "Beauty is truth, truth beauty." If Emily Dickinson is one
speaker, who might be her "brethren"? (A) Geoffrey Chaucer
(B) John Keats (C) Alexander Pope (D) Anne Bradstreet (E)
John Donne.

_22. Slant rhyme is employed by Emily Dickinson to empha-
size meaning by making which word stand out? (A) scarce
(B) Truth (C) Beauty (D) Tomb (E) Names.

Continuing questions on "I Died for Beauty -- but was scarce"

_23. All of the following are possible interpretations of the ambiguous idea "Beauty is truth -- truth beauty" EXCEPT:
(A) Dickinson preferred the beauty to the changing reality of life. (B) This statement characterizes the search for beauty that typifies most Romantic writing. (C) This statement is a universal and profound metaphysical proposition. (D) This statement is simply nonsense. (E) This is an overstatement uttered in the course of a dramatic dialogue.

_24. In the third stanza, moss literally may be growing in the cemetery setting of the poem, covering up the names, but figuratively, moss is also a metaphor for what? (A) Summer (B) Time (C) Age (D) Death (E) Life.

_25. Based on the beginning and ending lines of this poem, Dickinson's tone is (A) Pessimistic (B) Optimistic (C) Indifferent (D) Tremulous (E) Care-free.

_26. Which of the following best describes the poem as a whole? (A) An amusing satire on the excessive interest in Beauty and Truth. (B) A poetic expression of the need for love to give meaning to life. (C) A concisely written poem about the ambiguity of Beauty and Truth. (D) A personal meditation on human courage in the face of death. (E) A lyrical celebration of the importance of humanity's search for Beauty and Truth.

Questions 27 - 40. Read the following passage from "The Artifices of Tragedy" by Joseph Addison carefully before you choose your answers.

Among the several **artifices** which are put in practice by poets to fill the minds of an audience with terror, the first place is due to **thunder and lightning,** which are often made use of at the descending of a god or at the rising of a ghost, at the vanishing of a devil or at the death of a tyrant. I have known a bell introduced into several tragedies with good effect . . . but there is nothing which delights and terrifies our English theater so much as a ghost, especially when he appears in a bloody shirt. A specter has often saved a play though he has done nothing but stalked across the stage, or rose through a cleft of it and sunk again without speaking one word. There may be a **proper season** for these several terrors; and when they only come in as aids and assistances to the poet, they are not only to be excused, but to be applauded. . . .

For the moving of pity, our principal machine is the handkerchief; and indeed in our common tragedies, we should not know very often that the persons are in distress by anything they say, if they did not from time to time apply their handkerchiefs to their eyes. Far be it from me to think of banishing this instrument of sorrow from the stage; I know a tragedy could not subsist without it: All that I would contend for is to keep it from being misapplied. In a word, I would have the actor's tongue sympathize with his eyes.

A disconsolate mother with a child in her hand has frequently drawn compassion from the audience, and has therefore gained a place in several tragedies. A modern writer, that observed how this had took in other plays, being resolved to double the distress and melt his audience twice as much . . . brought a princess upon the stage with a little boy in one hand and a little girl in the other. This too had a very good effect. A third poet, being resolved to outwrite all his predecessors, a few years age introduced three children with great success. And, as I am informed, a young gentleman, who is fully determined to break the most obdurate hearts, has a tragedy by him where the first person that appears upon the stage is an afflicted widow in her mourning-weeds with half a dozen fatherless children attending her. . . . Thus several incidents that are beautiful in a good writer become ridiculous by falling into the hands of a bad one. But among all our methods of moving pity or terror, there is none so absurd and barbarous, and what more exposes us to the contempt and ridicule of our neighbors, than that dreadful butchering of one another that is so frequent upon the English stage. To delight in seeing men stabbed poisoned, racked, or impaled is certainly the sign of a cruel temper. . . .

It is indeed very odd to see our stage strewn with carcasses in the last scene of a tragedy; and to observe in the wardrobe of the playhouse several daggers, poniards, wheels, bowls for poison, and many other instruments of death. . . . To give my opinion upon this case; the fact ought not to have been represented but to have been told if there was any occasion for it.

_27. The word "artifices," as used in this passage, is synonymous with all BUT one of the following: (A) machine (B) instrument (C) trick (D) person (E) tactic.

_28. The phrases "thunder and lightning, which are often made use of at the descending of a god or at the rising of a ghost, at the vanishing of a devil or at the death of a tyrant" is an example of creating what type of sentence structure? (A) parallel (B) compound (C) simple (D) tight, simple (E) compound-complex.

_29. This passage is addressing what genre of literature? (A) comedies (B) tragedies (C) novels (D) short stories (E) poems.

_30. All BUT one of the following artifices is mentioned in par. 1: (A) thunder (B) lightning (C) handkerchiefs (D) ghosts (E) bells.

_31. Which statement by Addison indicates the "proper season" for these artifices? (A) when the "actor's tongue (does not) sympathize with his eyes" (B) "when they only come in as aids and assistances to the poet" (C) when the poet needs to show that "the persons are in distress" (D) when the poet is "fully determined to break the most obdurate hearts" (E) when the poet wants "to fill the minds of an audience with terror."

_32. The topic of par. 1 is: (A) terror (B) sorrow (C) humor (D) pity (E) B and D only.

_33. In the first paragraph, the author's attitude toward those who use artifices can be best described as (A) suspicious (B) critical (C) incredulous (D) admirable (E) uncertain.

_34. The topic of par 2 is: (A) terror (B) sorrow (C) humor (D) pity (E) B and D only.

_35. Beginning in third paragraph, Addison shifts his emphasis of praising artifices used in the proper way to (A) satirizing bad writers' use of artifices through his use of hyperbole (B) illustrating good writers' use of artifices through his use of imagery (C) exposing good writers' use of artifices through his use of similes (D) defining bad writers by their lack of artifices through his use of litotes (E) praising artifices used in the improper way.

_36. When Addison uses the word "poet" he means: (A) essayist (B) dramatist (C) diarist (D) biographer (E) critic.

_37. All of the following words show Addison's disapproval EXCEPT: (A) absurd (B) barbarous (C) assistance (D) impaled (E) racked.

_38. Addison use of the word "carcasses" in the last paragraph conveys a tone of (A) indifference (B) disgust (C) difference (D) ambivalence (E) disinterest.

_39. A poniard is all of the following EXCEPT (A) an instrument of death (B) a dagger (C) a knife (D) a medicinal instrument (E) and instrument of torture.

_40. Which of the following best describes the pattern of the author's discussion? (A) statement of fact followed by tentative assumptions (B) description of theory followed by exceptions to the theory (C) general statement followed by more general statements (D) forceful argumentation followed by concession to opponents (E) presentation of a problem followed by resolution of the problem.

Go on to the Fourth Passage

Questions 41 - 50. Read the following passage from Nathaniel Hawthorne's *The Scarlet Latter* carefully before you choose your answers.

Hester Prynne's term of confinement was now at an end. Her prison door was thrown open and she came forth into the sunshine, which, falling on all alike, seemed, to her sick and morbid heart, as if meant for no other purpose than to reveal the scarlet letter on her breast. Perhaps there was a more real torture in her first unattended footsteps from the threshold of the prison than even in the procession and spectacle that have been described, where she was made the common **infamy** at which all mankind was summoned to point its finger. Then, she was supported by an unnatural tension of the nerves and by all the combative energy of her character, which enabled her to convert the scene into a kind of **lurid** triumph.... The very law which condemned her -- a giant of stern features, but with vigor to support, as well as to annihilate, in his iron arm -- had held her up through the terrible ordeal of her **ignominy**. But now, with this unattended walk from the prison door, began the daily custom; and she must either sustain and carry it forward by the ordinary resources of her character, or sink beneath it. She could no longer borrow from the future to bear her present grief. Tomorrow would bring its own trial with it; so would the next day; and so would the next; each its own trial, and yet the very same that was now so unutterably grievous to be borne. The days of the far off future would toil onward; still with the same burden for her to take up and bear along with her, but never to fling down; for the accumulating days and added years would pile up their misery upon the heap of shame. Throughout them all, giving up her individuality, she would become the general symbol at which the preacher and moralist might point, and in which they might vivify and embody their images of woman's frailty and sinful passion. Thus, the young would be taught to look at her ... as the figure, the body, the reality of sin.

_41. Why does Hester have a "sick and morbid heart" (line 4)? (A) She hates the public (B) She has cardiovascular problems (C) She is experiencing guilt and confinement (D) The prison has made her sick. (E) She knows her husband is waiting.

_42. The phrase "the sunshine . . . (was) falling forth. . . as if meant . . . to reveal the scarlet letter on her breast" in lines 3 - 5 is an example of what figure of speech? (A) Personification (B) Allusion (C) Metaphor (D) Simile (E) Alliteration.

_43. The word "infamy" in line 9 of the above passage describes Hester as being a symbol of all but one the following: (A) shame (B) goodness (C) scandal (D) wickedness (E) atrocity.

_44. In lines 1 - 10 of this passage, what is going through Hester's head? (A) She feels everything is against her. (B) She thinks she must be crazy. (C) She is glad everything is finally over. (D) She is glad she is free at last. (E) She can't wait to get home.

_45. In line 12 of the above passage "lurid" means all but one of the following: (A) Pale (B) Sensational (C) Yellow (D) Racy (E) Exciting.

_46. The phrase "The very law which condemned her -- a giant of stern features, but with vigor to support, as well as to annihilate, in his iron arm - " in lines 13 - 15 is an example of a (A) Personification (B) Allusion (C) Metaphor (D) Simile (E) Alliteration.

_47. In line 16 of the above passage "ignominy" means all but one of the following: (A) Honor (B) Shame (C) Disgrace (D) Dishonor (E) Scandal.

_48. What type of poetical device is Hawthorne using in the phrase "The days of the far off future would toil onward. . . " in lines 23 - 24? (A) Personification (B) Allusion (C) Metaphor (D) Simile (E) Alliteration.

_49. The last sentence of this passage, "Thus, the young would be taught to look at her ... as the figure, the body, the reality of sin. . . ." is an example of (A) Personification (B) Allusion (C) Metaphor (D) Simile (E) Alliteration.

_50. Hester's attitude in this passage can be best described as (A) fearful acceptance of the morbid Puritan punishment allotted her (B) Reverence for God's people (C) Self-satisfaction with the human dominion over humans (D) Disgust with the evil that permeates Salem (E) Scorn at the Puritan harshness.

END OF SECTION I, PRACTICE TEST THREE

IF YOU FINISH BEFORE TIME IS CALLED,
YOU MAY CHECK YOUR WORK ON THIS SECTION

DO NOT GO ON UNTIL TOLD TO DO SO.

Practice Test 2:
"Use A PEN"

ENGLISH
LITERATURE AND COMPOSITION
SECTION II
Time - 2 hours
Number of questions - 3
Percent of total grade - 55

Each question counts as one-third of the total essay score.
Question 1 Essay -- Suggested time. . . . . 40 minutes
Question 2 Essay -- Suggested time. . . . . 40 minutes
Question 3 Essay -- Suggested time. . . . . 40 minutes

Section II of this examination requires answers in essay form. To help you use your time well, the coordinator will announce the time at which each question should be completed. If you finished any question before the time is announced, you may go on to the following question. If you finish the examination in less than the time allotted, you may go back and work on any essay you want.

The quality of the composition will be considered in the scoring of all essay questions. Essays will be judged on their clarity and effectiveness in dealing with the topics. In response to Question 3, select only a work of literary merit that will be appropriate to the question. A general rule of thumb is to use works of the same quality as those you have been reading during your Advanced Placements year(s).

After completing each question, you should check your essay for accuracy and punctuation, spelling, and diction; you Are advised, however, not to attempt many long corrections. Remember that quality is far more important than quantity.

You should write your essays with a pen, preferably in black or dark blue ink. If you must use a pencil, be sure it has a well-sharpened point. Be sure to write CLEARLY and LEGIBLY. Cross out any errors you make.

The questions for Section II are printed in the green insert. Use the green insert to organize your answers and for scratch work, but write your answers in the pink essay booklet. Answer questions in order and number each answer as the question is numbered in the examination. Do not skip lines. Begin each answer on a new page in the pink essay booklet.

Note: These directions are copied from the essay section of *The 1994 AP English Literature and Composition: Free-Response Scoring Guide with Multiple-Choice Section* © Copyright 1995 by College Entrance Examination Board and Educational Testing Service. All rights reserved.

ENGLISH LITERATURE AND COMPOSITION
SECTION II
Total Time -- 2 hours
Question I
(Suggested time — 40 minutes. This question
counts one-third of the total)

Prior to the beginning of the following excerpt from "Story of an Hour," great care has been taken to break to Mrs. Mallard the news that her husband had been killed in a car accident. As the story progresses, Kate Chopin, the author, seems to sympathize with Mrs. Mallard, despite the fact that her grieving over her husband's death is mixed with joy. Read the short story carefully. Then write a well-organized essay in which you analyze how Chopin uses such resources of language as descriptive diction, imagery, and figurative language to convey her attitude toward Mrs. Mallard.

She sat with her head thrown back upon the cushion of the chair, quite motionless, except when a sob came up into her throat and shook her, as a child who has cried itself to sleep continues to sob in its dreams.

She was young, with a fair, calm face, whose lines bespoke repression and even a certain strength. But now there was a dull stare in her eyes, whose gaze was affixed away off yonder on one of those patches of blue sky. It was not a glance of reflection, but rather indicated a suspension of intelligent thought.

There was something coming to her and she was waiting for it, fearfully. What was it? She did not know; it was too subtle and elusive to name. But she felt it, creeping out of the sky, reaching toward her through the sounds, the scents, the color that filled the air.

Now her bosom rose and fell tumultuously. She was beginning this thing that was approaching to possess her, and she was striving to beat it back with her will - as powerless as her two white slender hands would have been.

When she abandoned herself a little whispered word escaped her slightly parted lips. She said it over and over under her breath: "free, free, free!" The vacant stare and the look of terror that had followed it went with her eyes. They stayed keen and bright. Her pulses beat fast, and the coursing blood warmed and relaxed every inch of her body.

She did not stop to ask if it were or were not a monstrous joy that held her. A clear and exalted perception enabled her to dismiss the suggestion as trivial.

She knew that she would weep again when she saw the kind, tender hands folded in death; the face that had never looked save with love upon her, fixed and gray and dead. But she saw beyond that bitter moment a long procession of years to come that would belong to her absolutely. And she opened and spread her arms out to them in welcome.

There would be no one to live for during those coming years; she would live for herself. There would be no powerful will bending hers in that blind persistence with which men and women believe they have a right to impose a private will upon a fellow-creature. A kind intention or a cruel intention made the act seem no less a crime as she looked upon it in that brief moment of illumination. . . .

Josephine was kneeling before the closed door with her lips to the keyhole imploring for admission. . . .

"Go away. I am not making myself ill." No; she was drinking in a very elixir of life through that open window. . . .

She arose at length and opened the door to her sister's importunities. There was a feverish triumph in her eyes, and she carried herself unwittingly like a goddess of Victory. She clasped her sister's waist, and together they descended the stairs. Richards stood waiting for them at the bottom.

Someone was opening the front door with a latchkey. It was Brently Mallard who entered, a little travel-stained, composedly carrying his gripsack and umbrella. He had been far from the scene of the accident, and did not even know there had been one. He stood amazed at Josephine's piercing cry; at Richard's quick motion to screen him from the view of his wife.

But Richard's was too late.

When the doctors came they said she had died of heart disease - of joy that kills.

Question 2
(Suggested time - 40 minutes. This questions counts one-third of the total essay score.)

Read carefully the following poem by American poet, Emily Dickinson. Then write a well-organized essay in which you discuss how the central metaphor of stanza 2 and 3 expresses the complex attitude of the speaker.

I dwell in Possibility --

I dwell in Possibility --
A fairer House than Prose --
More numerous of Windows --
Superior -- for Doors --

(5)   Of Chambers as the Cedars --
Impregnable of Eye --
And for an Everlasting Roof --
The Gambrels of the Sky --

Of Visitors -- the fairest --
(10)   For Occupation -- This --
The spreading wide my narrow Hands
To gather Paradise --

Question 3
(Suggested time - 40 minutes. This questions counts
one-third of the total essay score.)

Some workers select unreliable narrators, whose interpretations of events are different from those of the author's. Select a work of literary merit in which the narrator, perhaps because of youth, lack of self knowledge, or lack of sophistication, could be considered unreliable. Then analyze how the choice of narration is artistically appropriate for the author's purpose.

Choose a novel by one of the following authors or another author of comparable merit.

Mark Twain	Chinua Achebe
Charles Dickens	James Baldwin
Harper Lee	Saul Bellow
J. D. Salinger	Joseph Conrad
Ralph Ellison	Zora Neal Hurston
Toni Morrison	Eudora Welty
Alice Walker	Virginia Woolf
Willa Cather	Richard Wright
Margaret Atwood	John Updike
Louise Erdich	Bernard Malamud
William Faulkner	F. Scot Fitzgerald

Answers and Explanations

To Practice Test 2:
Section II: Essay

Checklist for
Question 1

from Kate Chopin's "Story of an Hour"

STEP 1: Subtract one point for each item **not checked** from the checklist below:

___-___1. The writer demonstrates an awareness of the complexity of Chopin's attitude toward Mrs. Mallard, including a discussion of its irony.

___-___2. The writer analyzes how descriptive diction, imagery, and figurative language distinguish Chopin's attitude toward Mrs. Mallard.

___-___3. The thesis clearly shows the connection between Chopin's attitude toward Mrs. Mallard and the language devices used to convey that attitude.

___-___4. The writer makes apt (a minimum of three embedded bits of quotes per paragraph) and specific (detailed and appropriate) reference to the text.

___-___5. The writer offers a convincing interpretation of the irony of Chopin's sympathetic attitude toward Mrs. Mallard.

___-___6. The writer demonstrates an ability to read perceptively by saying something beyond the easy and obvious to grasp

___-___7. The writer demonstrates a control over the virtues of effective communication, including the language unique to literary criticism.

___-___8. The writer's organization is implicit and original, yet communicates a clear message.

___-___9. The writer's diction, sentence structure, and grammar aid in communicating a clear message.

MAXIMUM SCORE RESULTS: Grader 1 _____

MAXIMUM SCORE RESULTS: Grader 2 _____

STEP 2: Subtract one point from the results of step 1 for each item **checked** from the rubrics list below. NOTE: To avoid a negative number, you may not have any more checks here than the total on the left.

___-___1. The writer's definition of the attitude is oversimplified or vague or omits any discussion of its irony.

___-___2. The writer discusses the rhetorical and stylistic devices with limited purpose or with inappropriate examples.

___-___3. The connection between the evidence and the author's attitude is less clear than those of the top-scoring essays.

___-___4. The writer's use of quotes is awkward, inappropriate, or uninteresting.

___-___5. The writer misreads the meaning of the passage or simply paraphrases the passage with no reference to the language devices used.

___-___6. The writer's interpretation is not as persuasive as those of the highest scoring essays.

___-___7. The writer misuses the literary term(s) addressed in the question or omits them partially or entirely.

___-___8. The organization of this essay is less original or implicit than those of the top-scoring essays.

___-___9. The essay reveals consistent weakness in grammar and/or other basic elements of composition.

RESULTS:

Grader 1: _____ - _____ = _____

           Step 1 Score   Step 2 Score

Grader 2: _____ - _____ = _____

           Step 1 Score   Step 2 Score

Grader 1 Score + Grader 2 Score = _____

Above sum / divided by 2 =

Score for essay

Answers and Explanations

To Practice Test 4:
Section II: AP Rubrics

Rubrics for Question 1

from Kate Chopin's "Story of an Hour"

8-9   Essays earning a score of 8-9 show a clear understanding of how Chopin's use of the language and rhetorical devices reflect her sympathetic attitude toward Mrs. Mallard. The writer presents a clear and relevant thesis — correctly identifying the irony of Chopin's attitude — supported by apt and specific evidence from the passage. The organization of these high scoring essays is implicit and clear. Thoroughly convincing, this prose demonstrates the writer's ability to control a wide range of the elements of effective writing, including the language unique to literary criticism, but need not be without flaws.

6-7   Essays earning the score of 6-7 correctly identify Chopin's attitude and analyze adequately how she conveys that ironic view, but the thesis is less specific than the top-scoring essay. Typically they show how some language or rhetorical devices convey that view, but leave out at least one important element, making the evidence less convincing. The connection between the evidence and Chopin's attitude may also be less clear than the top-scoring essay. The organization is less implicit than those of the highest scoring essays. A few lapses in diction, syntax, or use of literary language may be present, but usually the prose of 6 essays convey their writers' ideas clearly.

5   Essays earning the score of 5 define Chopin's attitude, but do not address the irony implicit in the passage, Their analysis of how she conveys that view, while accurate, is also limited or inconsistently developed. The writer may simply name the attitude without discussing it or he/she may not aptly address the language or rhetorical devices Chopin uses to convey that mood. The thesis may be too simple or the evidence too brief to prove the writer's points. The organization follows a typical 5 paragraph model. A few lapses in diction or syntax may be present, but for the most part the prose of 5 essays convey their writers' ideas clearly.

3-4   Essays earning the score of 3-4 may not answer the entire question. Frequently they misrepresent Chopin's attitude, analyze stylistic elements with limited purpose or accuracy, or catalogue various stylistic elements in the passage without relating them to Chopin's attitude. The prose of 4 essays usually conveys their writers' ideas adequately, but may suggest inconsistent control over such elements of writing as literary language, organization, diction, and syntax.

1-2   Essays earning the score of 1-2 demonstrate little or no success in characterizing Chopin's view and in analyzing how it is conveyed. Some substitute a simpler task, such as paraphrasing the passage or discussing language and rhetorical elements in general. The paper may be unusually short and the prose of 2 papers may reveal consistent weakness in grammar or another of the basic elements of composition.

Answers and Explanations
To Practice Test 3:
Section II: Results
of Essay 3

Kate Chopin's "Story of an Hour"

1. The writer demonstrates an awareness of the complexity of Chopin's attitude toward Mrs. Mallard, including a discussion of its irony.

    A. Grief is a personal, unique and all-together terrifyingly complex emotion.

    B. In this essay by Kate Chopin, it seems quite ironic that Mrs. Mallard's grieving is mixed with some joy.

    C. In Chopin's passage, a wife's cycle of grieving is chronicled by an ironically sympathetic author.

2-3. The writer analyzes how the resources of language distinguish Chopin's attitude toward Mrs. Mallard. Besides descriptive diction, imagery, and figurative language some students picked other devices such as point of view, similes and pathos, but the important thing is to connect language back to the stem of the question. That is, connect the author's manipulation of the language to the creation of the attitude.

    A. "Chopin's ironically sympathetic attitude can be seen through her use of similes. (This gets a check but it is less perceptive than those of the higher scoring essays so it would also get a check on the left. In fact, if you use this organizational approach, the highest you will probably score is a 6)

    B. Kate Chopin sympathizes with Mrs. Mallard against marriage and the "persistence" with which it "imposes" on men and women. (The approach in B and C connects language to meaning in a more natural way, resulting in a higher score.)

    C. Describing Mrs. Mallard in terms contradictory to what is expected for a grieving widow creates a hidden irony.

4. The writer makes apt (a minimum of three embedded bits of quotes per paragraph) and specific (detailed and appropriate) reference to the text.

A. The "feverish triumph" in her eyes and the "brief moment of illumination" she felt, set her outside the reality of this moment.

5. The writer offers a convincing interpretation of the irony of Chopin's sympathetic attitude toward Mrs. Mallard.

A. Kate Chopin describes a woman who, at the height of her grief, can not decipher whether it is joy or sorrow she is feeling.

B. Although both grief-stricken and joyful, the author seems to admire Mrs. Mallard's independence.

6. The writer demonstrates an ability to read perceptively by saying something beyond the easy and obvious to grasp.

A. Somewhere the writer must mention how the empathy toward Mrs. Mallard sets the reader up for the surprise ending.

B. The metaphors present are positive, uplifting, and have nothing to do with death.

7. The writer demonstrates a control over the virtues of effective communication, including the language unique to literary criticism. Correct the following misuse of literary terms:

A. Kate Chopin picks descriptive terms contrary to the **genre** of a funeral day.

B. The author uses **allusion** to show how Mrs. Mallard sees things that are not there.

8. The writer's organization is implicit and original, yet communicates a clear message. The highest score will discuss the language of the passage in a natural way. Do not force an organization into every essay. Avoid topic sentences that name the device and make a connection to the attitude, yet say nothing specific:

A. The imagery shows the irony in the story.

B. Chopin's sympathy is shown through her use of similes.

9. The writer's diction, sentence structure, and grammar need to aid in communicating a clear message. Correct the following:

A. After receiving news of his death there was a vacant feeling in her being.

B. I will use descriptive diction, imagery, and figurative language to prove to you that Kate Chopin felt sympathy for Mrs. Mallard.

Answers and Explanations

To Practice Test 2:
Section II: Essay
Question 2

Checklist for Question 1   from "I dwell in Possibility"
by Emily Dickinson
STEP 1: Subtract one point for each item **not checked** from
the checklist below:

___-___1. The writer demonstrates a thorough understanding
of the speaker's complex attitude toward poetry.

___-___2. The writer analyzes how the poem's central metaphor expresses the speaker's complex attitude.

___-___3. The writer makes apt and specific references to "I
dwell in Possibility."

___-___4. The writer offers a convincing interpretation of "I
dwell in Possibility."

___-___5. The writer demonstrates an ability to read perceptively by making conclusions that are beyond the obvious and
easy to grasp.
___-___6. This essay adequately supports the discussion of
each language device by using a minimum of three embedded bits of quotes per paragraph.
___-___7. The writer demonstrates the hall marks of good writing by communicating a clear message through the use of implicit organization.
___-___8. The writer demonstrates consistent control over the
language unique to the criticism of literature.

___-___9. The diction, sentence structure, and grammar also
aid in communicating a clear message.

MAXIMUM SCORE RESULTS: Grader 1 _____

MAXIMUM SCORE RESULTS: Grader 2 _____

STEP 2: Subtract one point from the results of step 1 for each item **checked** from the rubrics list below. NOTE: To avoid a negative number, you may not have any more checks here than the total on the left.

___-___1. The writer's handling of the complex attitude of the speaker is less thorough or less precise than those of the higher scoring essays

___-___2. The writer's discussion of how the poem's central metaphor expresses the speaker's complex attitude is more vague, mechanical and briefer than those of the higher scoring essays.

___-___3. The writer's analysis is less well-supported and less incisive than those of the higher scoring essays.

___-___4. The writer's analysis has minor flaws in interpretation.

___-___5. The writer misses the complexity of Dickinson's poem.

___-___6. Although adequate in number, the evidence in this essay is not as convincing as the top-scoring essay.

___-___7. A few lapses in language unique to literary criticism may be present, but the message is clear.

___-___8. The organization of this essay is less appropriate than those of the top-scoring essays.

___-___9. The essay reveals consistent weakness in grammar and/or other basic elements of composition.

RESULTS:

Grader 1: _____ - _____ = _____
  Step 1 Score   Step 2 Score
Grader 2: _____ - _____ = _____
  Step 1 Score   Step 2 Score
Grader 1 Score + Grader 2 Score = _____

Above sum /
divided by 2 =

Score for essay

Answers and Explanations

To Practice Test 2:
Section II: AP Rubrics

Rubrics for Question 2

from Emily Dickinson's "I dwell in Possibility"

8-9   These well-written essays clearly demonstrate an understanding how the poem's central metaphor expresses the complex attitude of the speaker. In their references, they are apt and specific. Though not without flaws, these papers will offer a convincing interpretation of "I dwell in Possibility" and consistent control over the elements of effective composition. They demonstrate the writer's ability to write with clarity and skill.

6-7   These essays also demonstrate an understanding of Dickinson's poem; but, compared to the best essays, they are less thorough or less precise in their analysis of how the controlling metaphor expresses the complex attitude of the speaker. In addition to minor flaws in interpretation, their discussion is likely to be less well-supported and less incisive. These essays demonstrate the writer's ability to express ideas clearly, but with less mastery and control than the 8-9 papers.

5   These essays are characterized by superficiality. Their discussion of how the controlling metaphor expresses the complex attitude of the speaker may be vague, mechanical, or inadequately supported. They deal with the assigned tasks without important errors, but miss the complexity of Dickinson's poem. The writing is sufficient to convey the writer's thoughts, but these essays are typically pedestrian, not well-conceived, organized or developed as the upper-half papers. Often they reveal simplistic thinking and/or immature writing.

3-4   These lower half essays often reflect an incomplete or oversimplified understanding of the poem. Typically, they fail to respond to part(s) of the question. Their discussion may be meager, weak, or irrelevant, the controlling metaphor insufficiently identified, or the issues of complexity incompletely grasped; the discussion inaccurate or unclear. The writing demonstrates shaky control over the standard elements of college-level composition. These essays usually contain recurrent stylistic flaws and/or misreadings, and they often lack of persuasive evidence from the text.

1-2 These essay compound the weaknesses of the 3-4 range. They are marred by many infelicities: significant misinterpretations, insufficient development, and serious omissions. Frequently they are unacceptably brief. They are often poorly written on several counts, and may contain many distracting errors in grammar and mechanics. While some attempt has been made to answer the question, the writer's views are presented with little clarity.

0 This is a response with no more than a reference to the poem.

- Indicates a blank response, or is completely off-topic.

Answers and Explanations

To Practice Test 2:
Section II: Results
of Essay 2

Question 1
from "I dwell in Possibility"
by Emily Dickinson

1-2. The writer demonstrates a thorough understanding of how the controlling metaphor expresses the speaker's complex attitude.

    A. In the first two lines of the poem, the speaker names the house as a metaphor expressing the speaker's ambiguous preference for poetry over prose.

    B. The imagery employed throughout the poem compares poetry to prose as though they both were houses, each having their own windows, doors, chambers and roofs, but the house of poetry has more "possibilities."

    C. The imagery of the house progresses from comparisons of man made objects to nature objects to supernatural objects

3-6. The writer makes apt and specific references (a minimum of three embedded bits of quotes per paragraph) to "I dwell in Possibility," offering a convincing interpretation of the poem's meaning that demonstrates an ability to read perceptively by making conclusions that are beyond the obvious and easy to grasp.

    A. The Chambers of the house of poetry are made of "Cedar," known for it beauty, fragrance, and durability. It is "Impregnable of Eye --"

    B. The roof of the house of poetry is compared to the sky, but the qualifier, "Everlasting," raise it even higher.

    C. In the final two line the poet's comparison becomes even more expansive. She is able to spread wide her "narrow Hands/To Gather Paradise."

D. The house of Poetry is a better house because it offers more "Possibility" in the form of more numerous . . . windows . . . Doors . . . " and an "Everlasting Roof."

8-9. Correct the following mistakes in diction, sentence structure, or grammar:

A. There are many interpretations of the value of poetry in today's society.

B. Imagery is continuously used throughout the poem to convey meaning.

C. Within Dickinson's poem, the reader is drawn by his unique choice of words, and in this can take normal every day diction and produce a kaleidoscope of meanings

D. In the poem "I dwell in Possibilty" by Dickinson, many different ideas and definitions are thrown out for the reader to grasp.

E. The order in which Dickinson writes the poem is very jumpy.

Answers and Explanations

To Practice Test 2:
Section II: Essay

Checklist for

Question 3

Open Question on NAIVELY NARRATED NOVELS

Step One: Add one point for each item checked from the list. (Grader one should check column 1. Grader 2 should check column 2):

___-___ 1. The writer selects a suitable novel in which the narrator is considered to be unreliable.

___-___ 2. The writer presents a reasonable explanation of the purpose and meaning of the work.

___-___ 3. The writer effectively explains how the narrator's youth, lack of self-knowledge, or lack of sophistication makes him/her an unreliable narrator, whose interpretations are different from those of the author.

___-___ 4. The writer effectively explains how the choice of narration is artistically appropriate for the author's purpose.

___-___ 5. The writer makes apt and specific reference to the text.

___-___ 6. The writer avoids plot summary not relevant to the explanation of the role that narrator plays in telling the story.

___-___ 7. The writer discusses the literary work with sophistication, insight, and understanding.

___-___ 8. The writer's displays consistent control over the language unique to the discussion of narration.

___-___ 9. The writer's diction, sentence structure, organization, and grammar aid in communicating a clear message.

MAXIMUM SCORE RESULTS: Grader 1 _____

MAXIMUM SCORE RESULTS: Grader 2 _____

STEP 2: Subtract one point from the results of step 1 for each item **checked** from the rubrics list below. NOTE: To avoid a negative number, you may not have any more checks here than the total on the left.

___-___1. The writer's selection of a naively narrated novel is not as appropriate as those of the higher scoring essays.

___-___2. The writer's explanation of the meaning of the work is less thorough, less specific, or less perceptive than those of the higher scoring essays.

___-___3. The writer's explanation of how the narrator's youth, lack of self-knowledge, or lack of sophistication makes him/her an unreliable narrator, whose interpretations are different from those of the author, may be vague, underdeveloped, or misguided.

___-___4. The writer's explanation of how the choice of narration is artistically appropriate for the author's purpose may be less convincing, mechanical, or inadequately related to the work as a whole.

___-___5. The writer's reference to the text lack the specificity of the higher scoring essays.

___-___6. The writer simply paraphrases the meaning of the work with little reference to its symbolic significance.

___-___7. The writer says nothing beyond the easy and obvious to grasp.

___-___8. The writer misuses the literary term(s) necessary to the discussion of narration or omits them partially or entirely.

___-___9. The essay contains distracting errors in grammar and mechanics.   RESULTS:

Grader 1: _____ - _____ = _____
                    Step 1 Score   Step 2 Score

Grader 2: _____ - _____ = _____
                    Step 1 Score   Step 2 Score

r 2 Score = _____

Above sum /
divided by 2 =

Score for essay

Answers and Explanations

To Practice Test 2:
Section II: AP Rubrics

Rubrics for Question 3

Free Response on NAIVELY NARRATED NOVELS

8-9   These well-written essays choose a suitable novel in which the narrator is considered to be unreliable, and they explain convincingly how the narrator functions in the work. Superior papers will be specific in their references, cogent in their explications, and free of plot summary not directly relevant to the role that narration plays in the work. These essays may not be flawless, but they demonstrate the writer's ability to discuss a literary work with insight and understanding and to control a wide range of the elements of effective composition.

6-7   These essays also analyze an appropriate naive narrator from an acceptable work of literature; they discuss how the narrator's youth, lack of knowledge, or lack of sophistication makes him or her an unreliable narrator, but are less thorough, less perceptive, or less specific than 8-9 papers. They deal with how the choice of narration is artistically appropriate for the author's purpose, but are less convincing than are the best responses. These essays are well-written, but with less maturity and control than the top papers. They demonstrate the writer's ability to analyze a literary work, but they reveal a more limited understanding than do papers in the 8-9 range.

5   Superficiality characterizes these essays. They choose suitable narrators, but their explanation of how the choice of narration is artistically appropriate for the author's purpose is vague or oversimplified. Their discussion of meaning may be pedestrian, mechanical or inadequately related to the chosen symbolism. Typically, these essays reveal simplistic thinking and/or immature writing. They usually demonstrate inconsistent control over the elements of composition and are not as well-conceived, organized, or developed as the upper-half papers. The writing, however, is sufficient to convey the writer's ideas.

3-4   These lower half essays may choose an acceptable work, but fail to explain how the author's choice of narration affects the work. Their analysis of the importance of the naive narrator is likely to be unpersuasive, perfunctory, underdeveloped, or misguided. The meaning they adduce may be inaccurate or insubstantial and not clearly related to the chosen narrator. Part of the question may be omitted altogether. The writing may convey the writer's ideas, but it reveals weak control over such elements as diction, syntax, organization, or grammar. Typically, these essays contain significant misinterpretations of the question or the work they discuss; they also may contain little, if any, supporting evidence, and practice paraphrase and plot summary at the expense of analysis.

1-2   These essays compound the weaknesses of the papers in the 3-4 range. They seriously misread the novel, or seriously misinterpret the significance of the naive narrator's role. Frequently, they are unacceptably brief. Often poorly written on several counts, they may contain many distracting errors in grammar and mechanics. Although some attempt may have been made to answer the question, the writer's views typically are presented with little clarity, organization, coherence, or supporting evidence.

PRACTICE TEST 2 SCORING

NOTE: See separate teacher's guide addendum for answers and explanations for all multiple-choice tests in this book. Add the results of your scores below to determine your AP Grade:

Section I: Multiple-Choice (Total)

_____ - (.25 X _____) = _____ X 1.2273=_____

Number Correct	Number Wrong	Multiple-Choice Score	Weighted Score Section I

Section II: Free-Response

Writing: Essay 1: _____ X 3.0556 = _____
Do not round

Writing: Essay 2: _____ X 3.0556 = _____
Do not round

Writing: Essay 3: _____ X 3.0556 = _____
Do not round

Use CHECKLISTS or RUBRICS on the preceding pages to grade your essays.

Weighted Section II Score

Do not round

Composite Score:

_____ + _____ = _____

Weighted Multiple-Choice Score	Weighted Free-Response Score	**Composite**

Composite Score	AP Grade
150 - 107 (71%)	5
106 - 93 (62%)	4
92 - 74 (49%)	3
73 - 44 (29%)	2
43 - 0	1

Practice Test 3:

General
Instructions

ENGLISH LITERATURE
AND COMPOSITION

Three hours are allotted for this examination: 1 hour for Section I, which consists of multiple-choice questions, and 2 hours for Section II, which consists of essay questions. The multiple-choice questions are printed in this booklet; all essay questions are printed in a separate booklet.

SECTION I
Time — 1 hour
Number of questions - 50
Percent of total grade — 45

This examination contains 50 multiple-choice questions. Therefore, please be careful to fill in only the ovals that are preceded by numbers 1 through 50 on your answer sheet.

General Instructions

DO NOT OPEN THIS TEST BOOKLET UNTIL YOU ARE INSTRUCTED TO DO SO.

INDICATE ALL YOUR ANSWERS TO QUESTIONS IN SECTION I ON THE SEPARATE ANSWER SHEET. No credit will be given for anything written in this examination booklet, but you may use the booklet for notes or scratch work. After you have decided which of the suggested answers is best, COMPLETELY fill in the corresponding oval on the answer sheet. Give only one answer to each question. If you change an answer, be sure that the previous mark is erased completely.

Example: Sample Answer:

   Austin is a   A Ⓑ C D E

   (A) state
   (B) city
   (C) country
   (D) continent
   (E) village

Many candidates wonder whether or not to guess the answers
to questions about which they are not certain. In this section
of the examination, as a correction for haphazard guessing,
one-fourth of the number of questions you answer incorrectly
will be subtracted from the questions you answer correctly. It
is improbable, therefore, that mere guessing will improve your
score significantly; it may even lower your score, and it does
take time. If however you are not sure of the correct answer
but have some knowledge of the question and are able to eliminate one or more of the answer choices as wrong, your chance
of getting the right answer is improved, and it may be to your
advantage to answer such a question.

Use your time effectively, working as rapidly as you can without losing accuracy. Do not spend too much time on questions
that are too difficult. Go on to other questions and come back
to the difficult ones later if you have time. It is not expected
that everyone will be able to answer all the multiple-choice
questions.

Note: These directions are copied from the multiple-choice
section of *The 1994 Advanced Placement Examination in English
Literature and Composition: Free-Response Scoring Guide with
Multiple-Choice Section.* Copyright © 1995 by College Entrance
Examination Board and Educational Testing Service. All rights
reserved.

Practice Test 3:

General Instructions

ENGLISH LITERATURE
AND COMPOSITION
SECTION I -- Time -- 1 hour

<u>Directions:</u> This section consists of literary works and questions on their content, form, and style. After reading each passage, choose the best answer to each question and fill in the corresponding oval on the answer sheet.

<u>Note:</u> Pay particular attention to the requirement of questions that contain the words NOT, LEAST, or EXCEPT.

<u>Question 1-8.</u> Read the following poem by Dylan Thomas carefully before choosing your answers.

> Do not go gentle into that good night,
> Old age should burn and rage at close of day;
> Rage, rage against the dying of the light.
>
> Though wise men at their end know dark is right,
> (5)   Because their words had forked no lightning they
> Do not go gentle into that good night.
>
> Good men, the last wave by, crying how bright
> Their frail deeds might have danced in a green bay,
> Rage, rage against the dying of the light.
>
> (10)   Wild men who caught and sang the sun in flight,
> And learn, too late, they grieved it on its way,
> Do not go gentle into that good night.
>
> Grave men, near death, who see with blinding sight
> Blind eyes could blaze like meteors and be gay,
> (15)   Rage, rage against the dying of the light.
> And you, my father, there on the sad height,
> Curse, bless, me now with you fierce tears, I pray.
> Do not go gentle into that good night.
> Rage, rage against the dying of the light.

_1. All BUT one of the following are characteristics of a villanelle, a French verse form, and are true of this poem: (A) The poem consists of five tercets and a concluding quatrain. (B) The poem employs only three end rhymes. (C) The first and third lines alternately conclude the tercets. (D) The first and third lines form a concluding couplet for the quatrain. (E) The rhyme scheme of each tercet is *aba*.

_2. Despite the villanelle's restrictions, Dylan Thomas's poem is remarkably (A) repetitious (B) restricted (C) unforced (D) formal (E) effusive.

_3. The speaker in this poem can be characterized as one who (A) loves life (B) believes in in "after-life" (C) believes death is only a gateway to heaven (D) does not want his father to die (E) does not believe in heaven.

_4. Variety is achieved through all BUT one of the following metonymies for death: (A) "good night" - lines 1, 6, 12, 18 (B) "close of day" - line 2 (C) "dying of the light" - lines 3, 9, 15, 19 (D) "dark" - line 4 (E) " a green bay" - line 8.

_5. The following pun is used by Thomas to attach two different meanings to the same word: (A) "wise" men - line 4 (B) "good" men - line 7 (C) "wild" men - line 10 (D) "grave" men - line 13 (E) my "father" - line 16.

_6. The following oxymoron used by Thomas creates an unusual image by combining opposite terms: (A) "should burn and rave at the close of day" - line 2 (B) "their words had no forked lightning" - line 5 (C) "might have danced in a green bay" - line 8 (D) "caught and sang the sun" - line 10 (E) "who see with blinding sight" - line 13.

_7. The figure of speech which dominates the poem is the overall form of the (A) apostrophe (B) simile (C) metaphor (D) pun (E) oxymoron.

_8. Thomas introduces all BUT one of the following people in the poem who might be expected to accept death gently but who, nonetheless, resist it: (A) Philosophers (B) Theologians (C) Factory Workers (D) Inspired artists (E) writers.

<u>Question 9 - 15.</u> Read the following poem by Dylan Thomas carefully before choosing your answers.

        Do not go gentle into that good night,
        Old age should burn and rage at close of day;
        Rage, rage against the dying of the light.

        Though wise men at their end know dark is right,
(5)   Because their words had forked no lightning they
        Do not go gentle into that good night.

        Good men, the last wave by, crying how bright
        Their frail deeds might have danced in a green bay,
        Rage, rage against the dying of the light.

(10)   Wild men who caught and sang the sun in flight,
        And learn, too late, they grieved it on its way,
        Do not go gentle into that good night.

        Grave men, near death, who see with blinding sight
        Blind eyes could blaze like meteors and be gay,
(15)   Rage, rage against the dying of the light.
        And you, my father, there on the sad height,
        Curse, bless, me now with you fierce tears, I pray.
        Do not go gentle into that good night.
        Rage, rage against the dying of the light.

_9. In the context of lines 4-6, "forked no lightning" means that wise men at the end regret that their words have (A) caused too much damage (B) created no radical change (C) lit up too many minds (D) glowed for too long (E) destroyed too many things.

_10. In the context of line 8, "danced in a green bay" means that good men at their end realize regretfully that their frail deeds might have been more productive if that had been performed (A) in a ballroom dance hall (B) for more envious people (C) for more unfortunate farmers (D) in a more fertile field (E) on a more colorful floor.

_11. How many types of people are addressed by Dylan Thomas as those who want to prolong their life and live it according to their new insights? (A) three (B) four (C) five (D) six (E) seven.

_12. The overall effect of the poem's metaphorical descriptions of death is to (A) internalize death and increase it's mystery (B) terrorize death and increase its threat (C) familiarize death and lessen its threat (D) abstract death and decrease its acceptance (E) externalize death and lessen its wonder.

_13. All BUT one of the following words are used by Dylan Thomas to convey a hopeful tone: (A) "good" (B) "right" (C) "bright" (D) "green" (E) "flight."

_14. All BUT one of the following words are used by Dylan Thomas to convey a regretful tone: (A) "dying" (B) "danced" (C) "dark" (D) "crying" (E) "grieved."

_15. A third layer of tone, fierce unacceptance, is added by Dylan Thomas's use of all of the following words EXCEPT: (A) "burn" (B) "rave" (C) "rage" (D) "wave" (E) "blaze."

Question 16 - 19. Read the following passage from the first half of Section I of Stephen Crane's *The Bride Comes to Yellow Sky* carefully before choosing your answers.

The great Pullman was whirling onward with such dignity of motion that a glance from the window seemed simply to prove that the plains of Texas were pouring eastward. Vast flats of green grass, dull-hued spaces of mesquite and cactus, little groups of frame houses, woods of light and tender trees, all were sweeping into the east, sweeping over the horizon, a precipice.

A newly married pair had boarded this coach at San Antonio. The man's face was reddened from many days in the wind and sun, and a direct result of his new black clothes was that his brick-colored hands were constantly performing in a conscious fashion. From time to time he looked down respectfully at his new attire. He sat with a hand on each knee, like a man waiting in a barber shop. The glances he devoted to other passengers were furtive and shy.

The bride was not pretty, nor was she very young. She wore a dress of blue cashmere, with small reservations of velvet here and there, and with steel buttons abounding. She continually twisted her head to regard her puff sleeves, very stiff, straight and high. They embarrassed her. It was quite apparent that she had cooked, and that she was expected to cook, dutifully. The blushes caused by the careless scrutiny of some passengers as she had entered the car were strange to see upon this plain, under-class countenance, which was drawn in placid, almost emotionless lines.

They were evidently very happy. . . .

Later he explained to her about the trains. "You see, it's a thousand miles from one end of Texas to the other; and this train runs right across it, and never stops but four times." He had the pride of an owner. He pointed out to her the dazzling fittings of the coach; and in truth her eyes opened wider as she contemplated the sea-green figured velvet, the shining brass, silver, and glass, the wood that gleamed as darkly brilliant as the surface of a pool of oil. At one end a bronze figure sturdily held a support for a separated chamber, and at convenient places on the ceiling were frescos in olive and silver.

To the minds of the pair, their surroundings reflected the glory of their marriage that morning in San Antonio; this

was the environment of their new estate; and the man's face, in particular, beamed with an elation that made him appear ridiculous to the Negro porter.

_16. All of the following, seen in the passage, are stereotypical elements seen in all Western stories EXCEPT: (A) The means of transportation is a "great Pullman " (B) The setting includes "Vast flats of green grass, dull-hued spaces of mesquite and cactus, little groups of frame houses" (C) "The man's face was reddened from many days in the wind and sun" (D) The man had "brick-colored hands" (E) The bride's new dress of blue cashmere was personified as having "small reservations of velvet here and there."

_17. All BUT one of the following characteristics, seen in the passage, make Stephen Crane's story a work of literary merit, rather than just a typical Western: (A) The train is personified as having "dignity of motion." (B) The man is described as "furtive and shy." (C) "The bride was not pretty, nor was she very young." (D) " It was quite apparent that she had cooked, and that she was expected to cook, dutifully" (E) "The blushes that were caused by the careless scrutiny of passengers . . . were strange to see upon this . . . underclass countenance."

_18. The Texas landscape in paragraph one is depicted with the following contrasting images
     I. " Green grass" and "dull-hued spaces"
     II. "Vast flats" and "green grass"
     III. "Little groups of frame houses" and "woods of light and tender trees"
(A) I only (B) II only (C) III only (D) I and III only (E) I, II, III

_19. All of the following phrases describing the bride were carefully chosen by Stephen Crane to elicit a multitude of images EXCEPT: (A) "careless scrutiny of some passengers" (B) "as she had entered the car" (C) "were strange to see" (D) "plain, under-class countenance" (E) "placid, almost emotionless lines."

Question 20 - 24. Read the following passage from the first half of Section I of Stephen Crane's *The Bride Comes to Yellow Sky* carefully before choosing your answers.

The great Pullman was whirling onward with such dignity of motion that a glance from the window seemed simply to prove that the plains of Texas were pouring eastward. Vast flats of green grass, dull-hued spaces of mesquite and cactus, little groups of frame houses, woods of light and tender trees, all were sweeping into the east, sweeping over the horizon, a precipice.

A newly married pair had boarded this coach at San Antonio. The man's face was reddened from many days in the wind and sun, and a direct result of his new black clothes was that his brick-colored hands were constantly performing in a conscious fashion. From time to time he looked down respectfully at his new attire. He sat with a hand on each knee, like a man waiting in a barber shop. The glances he devoted to other passengers were furtive and shy.

The bride was not pretty, nor was she very young. She wore a dress of blue cashmere, with small reservations of velvet here and there, and with steel buttons abounding. She continually twisted her head to regard her puff sleeves, very stiff, straight and high. They embarrassed her. It was quite apparent that she had cooked, and that she was expected to cook, dutifully. The blushes caused by the careless scrutiny of some passengers as she had entered the car were strange to see upon this plain, under-class countenance, which was drawn in placid, almost emotionless lines.

They were evidently very happy. . . .

Later he explained to her about the trains. "You see, it's a thousand miles from one end of Texas to the other; and this train runs right across it, and never stops but four times." He had the pride of an owner. He pointed out to her the dazzling fittings of the coach; and in truth her eyes opened wider as she contemplated the sea-green figured velvet, the shining brass, silver, and glass, the wood that gleamed as darkly brilliant as the surface of a pool of oil. At one end a bronze figure sturdily held a support for a separated chamber, and at convenient places on the ceiling were frescos in olive and silver.

To the minds of the pair, their surroundings reflected the glory of their marriage that morning in San Antonio; this

was the environment of their new estate; and the man's face, in particular, beamed with an elation that made him appear ridiculous to the Negro porter.

_20. The following oxymoron used by Crane creates an unusual image by combining opposite terms: (A) "sea-green figured velvet" (B) "shining brass, silver, and glass" (C) "the wood . . . gleamed . . . darkly brilliant " (D) "the surface of a pool of oil" (E) "frescos in olive and silver."

_21. The couple's attitude in these first paragraphs can be described as (A) embarrassed happiness (B) embittered sarcasm (C) elevated authority (D) inquisitive detachment (E) personal reminiscence.

_22. Which of the following phrases most pointedly refer to Jack's "private" nature? (A) "The man's face was reddened from many days in the wind and sun" (B) " A direct result of his new black clothes was that his brick-colored hands were constantly performing in a conscious fashion." (C) "From time to time he looked down respectfully at his new attire." (D) "He sat with a hand on each knee, like a man waiting in a barber shop." (E) "The glances he devoted to other passengers were furtive and shy."

_23. The phrase "it's a thousand miles from one end of Texas to the other; and this train runs right across it, and never stops but four times" is an example of which of the following? (A) A euphemism for the depravity of the Old West (B) An exaggeration of a common truth in Jack's life (C) An ironic reference to the price Jack had to pay for their train ride (D) An allusion to other commonly known Western stories (E) A suggestion that Jack perversely took delight in scaring his bride.

_24. In paragraph three, which of the following phrases best describe the origin of the brides embarrassment? (A) "The bride was not pretty, nor was she very young. (B) "She wore a dress of blue cashmere, with small reservations of velvet" (C) "It was quite apparent that she had cooked, and that she was expected to cook, dutifully." (D) The passengers regarded her with "careless scrutiny" . . . as she entered the car (E) She is described by the narrator as being "under-class."

Question 25 - 27. Read the following passage from the first half of Section I of Stephen Crane's *The Bride Comes to Yellow Sky* carefully before choosing your answers.

The great Pullman was whirling onward with such dignity of motion that a glance from the window seemed simply to prove that the plains of Texas were pouring eastward. Vast flats of green grass, dull-hued spaces of mesquite and cactus, little groups of frame houses, woods of light and tender trees, all were sweeping into the east, sweeping over the horizon, a precipice.

A newly married pair had boarded this coach at San Antonio. The man's face was reddened from many days in the wind and sun, and a direct result of his new black clothes was that his brick-colored hands were constantly performing in a conscious fashion. From time to time he looked down respectfully at his new attire. He sat with a hand on each knee, like a man waiting in a barber shop. The glances he devoted to other passengers were furtive and shy.

The bride was not pretty, nor was she very young. She wore a dress of blue cashmere, with small reservations of velvet here and there, and with steel buttons abounding. She continually twisted her head to regard her puff sleeves, very stiff, straight and high. They embarrassed her. It was quite apparent that she had cooked, and that she was expected to cook, dutifully. The blushes caused by the careless scrutiny of some passengers as she had entered the car were strange to see upon this plain, under-class countenance, which was drawn in placid, almost emotionless lines.

They were evidently very happy. . . .

Later he explained to her about the trains. "You see, it's a thousand miles from one end of Texas to the other; and this train runs right across it, and never stops but four times." He had the pride of an owner. He pointed out to her the dazzling fittings of the coach; and in truth her eyes opened wider as she contemplated the sea-green figured velvet, the shining brass, silver, and glass, the wood that gleamed as darkly brilliant as the surface of a pool of oil. At one end a bronze figure sturdily held a support for a separated chamber, and at convenient places on the ceiling were frescos in olive and silver.

To the minds of the pair, their surroundings reflected the glory of their marriage that morning in San Antonio; this

was the environment of their new estate; and the man's face, in particular, beamed with an elation that made him appear ridiculous to the Negro porter.

_25. The style of the passage as a whole can best be described as (A) humorless and pedantic (B) metaphorical and descriptive (C) ornate and archaic (D) effusive and complex (E) terse and epigrammatic.

_26. In paragraph five, the attention that the narrator pays to the details of the coach serves primarily to (A) construct a metaphor for the glory of the couple's marriage (B) divert the reader's attention from Jack's point of view (C) retard the pace of the narration prior to the climax (D) counter earlier reference to the vastness of Texas (E) offer a parallel to the transformation the Negro porter undergoes in the passage.

_27. All of the following words indicate the couple's attitude EXCEPT: (A) Furtive (B) Shy (C) Embarrassed (D) Careless (E) Happy.

Question 28 - 31. Read the following passage from the second half of Section I of Stephen Crane's *The Bride Comes to Yellow Sky* carefully before choosing your answers.

To the left, miles down a long purple slope, was a little ribbon of mist where moved the keening Rio Grande. The train was approaching it at an angle, and the apex was Yellow Sky. Presently it was apparent that, as the distance from Yellow sky grew shorter, the husband became commensurately restless. His brick-red hands were more insistent in their prominence. Occasionally he was even rather absentminded and faraway when the bride leaned forward and addressed him.

As a matter of truth, Jack Potter was beginning to find the shadow of a deed weigh upon him like a leaden slab. He, the town marshal of Yellow Sky, a man known, liked, and feared in his corner, a prominent person, had gone to San Antonio to meet a girl he believed he loved, and there, after the usual prayers, had actually induced her to marry him, without consulting Yellow Sky for any part of the transaction. He was now bringing his bride before an innocent and unsuspecting community.

Of course people in Yellow Sky married as it pleased them in accordance with a general custom; but such was Potter's thought of his duty to his friends, or their idea of his duty, or of an unspoken form which does not control men in these matters, and he felt he was heinous. He had committed an extraordinary crime. Face to face with this girl in San Antonio, and spurred by his sharp impulse, he had gone headlong over all the social hedges. At San Antonio he was like a man hidden in the dark. A knife to sever ant duty, any form, was easy to his hand in that remote city. But the hour of Yellow Sky -- the hour of daylight -- was approaching.

He knew full well that his marriage was an important thing to his town. It could only be exceeded by the burning of the new hotel. His friends could not forgive him. Frequently he had reflected on the advisability of telling them by telegraph, but a new cowardice had been upon him. He feared to do it. And now the train was hurrying him toward a scene of amazement, glee, and reproach. He glanced out the window at a line of haze swinging slowly in toward the train. . . .

He resolved that he would use all the devises of speed and plainscraft in making the journey from the station to his

house. Once within the safe citadel, he could issue some sort of vocal bulletin, and then not go among the citizens until they had time to wear off a little of their enthusiasm.

The bride looked anxiously at him. "What's worrying you, Jack?"

He laughed again. "I'm not worrying girl; I'm only thinking of Yellow Sky."

She flushed in comprehension.

A sense of mutual guilt invaded their minds and developed a finer tenderness. They looked at each other with eyes softly aglow. But Potter often laughed the same laugh; the flush upon the bride's face seemed permanent.

The traitor to the feelings of Yellow Sky narrowly watched the speeding landscape. "We're nearly there," he said.

_28. In the context of the first sentence, the word "keening" is best interpreted to mean (A) howling (B) piercing (C) biting (D) marvelous (E) great.

_29. In the context of the first sentence of the second paragraph, "the shadow of the deed" refers to his (A) restlessness (B) town, Yellow Sky (C) young bride (D) new marriage (E) beloved Rio Grande.

_30. In the sentence beginning "He, the town marshal of Yellow Sky, a man known, liked, and feared in his corner, a prominent person ..." Crane includes a lot of information about the main character through the use of (A) parallel construction (B) periodic thoughts (C) balanced descriptions (D) tight and simple sentence construction (E) loose sentence construction.

_31. Jack Potter's change in attitude from embarrassed happiness to restlessness can be best attributed to which of the following factors? (A) "To the left, miles down a long purple slope, was a little ribbon of mist where moved the keening Rio Grande." (B) "The train was approaching it at an angle, and the apex was Yellow Sky." (C) " His brick-red hands were more insistence in their prominence." (D) He was "the town marshal of Yellow Sky." (E) He had married without consulting Yellow Sky for any part of the transaction.

Question 32 - 35. Read the following passage from the second
half of Section I of Stephen Crane's *The Bride Comes to Yellow
Sky* carefully before choosing your answers.

To the left, miles down a long purple slope, was a little
ribbon of mist where moved the keening Rio Grande. The
train was approaching it at an angle, and the apex was Yellow
Sky. Presently it was apparent that, as the distance from Yellow sky grew shorter, the husband became commensurately
restless. His brick-red hands were more insistent in their prominence. Occasionally he was even rather absentminded and
faraway when the bride leaned forward and addressed him.

As a matter of truth, Jack Potter was beginning to find
the shadow of a deed weigh upon him like a leaden slab. He,
the town marshal of Yellow Sky, a man known, liked, and
feared in his corner, a prominent person, had gone to San Antonio to meet a girl he believed he loved, and there, after the
usual prayers, had actually induced her to marry him, without consulting Yellow Sky for any part of the transaction. He
was now bringing his bride before an innocent and unsuspecting community.

Of course people in Yellow Sky married as it pleased
them in accordance with a general custom; but such was
Potter's thought of his duty to his friends, or their idea of his
duty, or of an unspoken form which does not control men in
these matters, and he felt he was heinous. He had committed
an extraordinary crime. Face to face with this girl in San Antonio, and spurred by his sharp impulse, he had gone headlong
over all the social hedges. At San Antonio he was like a man
hidden in the dark. A knife to sever any duty, any form, was
easy to his hand in that remote city. But the hour of Yellow
Sky -- the hour of daylight -- was approaching.

He knew full well that his marriage was an important
thing to his town. It could only be exceeded by the burning of
the new hotel. His friends could not forgive him. Frequently
he had reflected on the advisability of telling them by telegraph, but a new cowardice had been upon him. He feared to
do it. And now the train was hurrying him toward a scene of
amazement, glee, and reproach. He glanced out the window
at a line of haze swinging slowly in toward the train. . . .

He resolved that he would use all the devises of speed
and plainscraft in making the journey from the station to his

house. Once within the safe citadel, he could issue some sort of vocal bulletin, and then not go among the citizens until they had time to wear off a little of their enthusiasm.

The bride looked anxiously at him. "What's worrying you, Jack?"

He laughed again. "I'm not worrying girl; I'm only thinking of Yellow Sky."

She flushed in comprehension.

A sense of mutual guilt invaded their minds and developed a finer tenderness. They looked at each other with eyes softly aglow. But Potter often laughed the same laugh; the flush upon the bride's face seemed permanent.

The traitor to the feelings of Yellow Sky narrowly watched the speeding landscape. "We're nearly there," he said.

_32. The phrase that describes the most ambiguous reason for the marshal's restlessness is (A) " He was now bringing his bride before an innocent and unsuspecting community."
(B) It "was Potter's thought of his duty to his friends" (C) It was "of an unspoken form which does not control men in these matters." (D) It was "their idea of his duty" (E) "He felt he was heinous."

_33. All of the following are synonyms for Yellow Sky's expected reaction to Jack's marriage, EXCEPT: (A) Incredulity (B) Stupefaction (C) Laughter (D) Indifference (E) Scandal.

_34. In this passage, image of "leaden slab" and "A knife to sever any duty" are contrasted with (A) the rigors of travel (B) manly fortitude (C) a " developed . . . finer tenderness" and "eyes softly aglow" (D) women and fashion (E) a "heinous. . . . and extraordinary crime."

_35. "His brick-red hands were more insistent in their prominence" is an example of (A) Personification (B) Onomatopoeia (C) Apostrophe (D) Antithesis (E) Simile.

Question 36 - 37. Read the following passage from the second half of Section I of Stephen Crane's *The Bride Comes to Yellow Sky* carefully before choosing your answers.

To the left, miles down a long purple slope, was a little
ribbon of mist where moved the keening Rio Grande. The
train was approaching it at an angle, and the apex was Yellow
Sky. Presently it was apparent that, as the distance from Yellow sky grew shorter, the husband became commensurately
restless. His brick-red hands were more insistent in their prominence. Occasionally he was even rather absentminded and
faraway when the bride leaned forward and addressed him.

As a matter of truth, Jack Potter was beginning to find
the shadow of a deed weigh upon him like a leaden slab. He,
the town marshal of Yellow Sky, a man known, liked, and
feared in his corner, a prominent person, had gone to San Antonio to meet a girl he believed he loved, and there, after the
usual prayers, had actually induced her to marry him, without consulting Yellow Sky for any part of the transaction. He
was now bringing his bride before an innocent and unsuspecting community.

Of course people in Yellow Sky married as it pleased
them in accordance with a general custom; but such was
Potter's thought of his duty to his friends, or their idea of his
duty, or of an unspoken form which does not control men in
these matters, and he felt he was heinous. He had committed
an extraordinary crime. Face to face with this girl in San Antonio, and spurred by his sharp impulse, he had gone headlong
over all the social hedges. At San Antonio he was like a man
hidden in the dark. A knife to sever any duty, any form, was
easy to his hand in that remote city. But the hour of Yellow
Sky -- the hour of daylight -- was approaching.

He knew full well that his marriage was an important
thing to his town. It could only be exceeded by the burning of
the new hotel. His friends could not forgive him. Frequently
he had reflected on the advisability of telling them by telegraph, but a new cowardice had been upon him. He feared to
do it. And now the train was hurrying him toward a scene of
amazement, glee, and reproach. He glanced out the window
at a line of haze swinging slowly in toward the train. . . .

He resolved that he would use all the devises of speed
and plainscraft in making the journey from the station to his

house. Once within the safe citadel, he could issue some sort of vocal bulletin, and then not go among the citizens until they had time to wear off a little of their enthusiasm.

The bride looked anxiously at him. "What's worrying you, Jack?"

He laughed again. "I'm not worrying girl; I'm only thinking of Yellow Sky."

She flushed in comprehension.

A sense of mutual guilt invaded their minds and developed a finer tenderness. They looked at each other with eyes softly aglow. But Potter often laughed the same laugh; the flush upon the bride's face seemed permanent.

The traitor to the feelings of Yellow Sky narrowly watched the speeding landscape. "We're nearly there," he said

_36. The chief subject treated in this passage is (A) A nostalgia for Yellow Sky (B) The uncertainties of Yellow Sky's reception of Jack and his new bride (C) The delights of marriage that Jack and his wife will enjoy (D) The bride's timid, self-pitying state of mind (E) Jack's view of himself in relationship to his new bride.

_37. Mirroring Jack's apprehension, the pace of the passage is quickened by the image of all BUT one of the following (A) the speeding landscape (B) the permanence of the bride's blush (C) The sense of mutual guilt that invaded the couple's minds (D) The sense of a finer tenderness that was developed in the couple (E) The narrator's choice of the word traitor to describe Jack Potter.

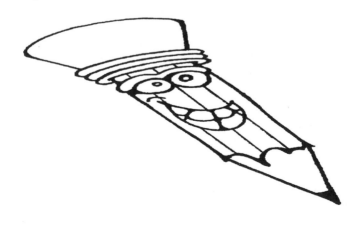

Question 38 - 44. Read the following poem *On First Looking into Chapman's Homer* by John Keats carefully before choosing your answers.

On First Looking into Chapman's Homer

Much have I traveled in the realms of gold,
And many goodly states and kingdoms seen;
Round many western islands have I been
Which bards in fealty to Apollo hold.
(5)　Oft of one wide expanse had I been told
That deep-browed Homer ruled as his demesne,
Yet did I never breathe its pure serene
Till I heard Chapman speak out loud and bold:
Then felt I like some watcher of the skies
(10)　When a new planet swims into his ken;
Or like stout Cortez when with eagles eyes
He stared at the Pacific -- and all his men
Looked at each other with a wild surmise --
Silent, upon a peak in Darien.

Line 4 - **Apollo** - Greek god of poetry . . . Line 6 - **demesne** - estate . . . Line 7 - **serene** - atmosphere . . . Line 10 - **ken** - range of sight . . . Line 11- **Cortez** - Vasco Nunez de Balboa, not Hernando Cortez, was the first European to sight the Pacific from Darien, a peak in Panama.

_38. This poem is concerned with all the following EXCEPT: (A) Reading as a method of imaginative discovery (B) Personal experience as a symbol for any discovery (C) Keats's personal discovery of Chapman's Homer (D) Cortez's discovery of the Pacific Ocean (E) The importance of imaginative discovery through reading.

_39. The controlling metaphor for discovery in the poem is built around a comparison of reading with (A) Writing (B) Traveling (C) Science (D) Physics (E) Medicine.

_40. Written as a Italian sonnet, John Keats had to follow the formal organization established by all of the following rules for a sonnet EXCEPT: (A) The ideas in the poem must be expressed in 14 lines, no more or no less. (B) Each line has to consist of 10 syllables (C) The meter has to be iambic pentameter (D) The verse has to be unrhymed. (E) The sonnet has to be organized into two unequal parts, an octave and a sestet.

_41. As an Italian sonnet, the reader has certain expectations for how meaning will be formed. Which of the following possibilities have been chosen by John Keats? (A) The octave presents a problem, the sestet a solution. (B) The octave and the sestet present the same problem from two different views. (C) The problem of the octave is intensified in the sestet, and no solution is given. (D) The octave presents a situation and a sestet describes a change in the situation. (E) The octave and the sestet presents different types of changes.

_42. In the octave, the speaker writes that he has " traveled in the realms of gold," and seen "many goodly states and kingdoms." Given the context of the rest of the poem, we know that the speaker is referring to his (A) Wide reading in the literature of Western civilization (B) Many travels to the western islands (C) Vast study of our planet system (D) Intense concern for the Preservation of eagles. (E) Accurate research on explorers.

_43. Examples of formal and dignified diction, used by John Keats to represent his respectful but dispassionate reading before discovering Chapman's Homer, include all BUT which of the following? (A) "goodly states" (B) "bards of fealty" (C) "had I been told" (D) "demesne" (E) "serene."

_44. A "turn" occurs between the octave and the sestet when the speaker describes the impact that reading Chapman's Homer has had on him. Images of exploration give way to (A) More intensified images of exploration (B) Images of discovery (C) Questions about the necessity of exploration (D) Answers to the questions about exploration previously made (E) Explanations for the necessity of exploration.

Question 45 - 50. Read the following poem *On First Looking into Chapman's Homer* by John Keats carefully before choosing your answers.

On First Looking into Chapman's Homer

Much have I traveled in the realms of gold,
And many goodly states and kingdoms seen;
Round many western islands have I been
Which bards in fealty to Apollo hold.
(5)   Oft of one wide expanse had I been told
That deep-browed Homer ruled as his demesne,
Yet did I never breathe its pure serene
Till I heard Chapman speak out loud and bold:
Then felt I like some watcher of the skies
(10)   When a new planet swims into his ken;
Or like stout Cortez when with eagles eyes
He stared at the Pacific -- and all his men
Looked at each other with a wild surmise --
Silent, upon a peak in Darien.

Line 4 - **Apollo** - Greek god of poetry . . . Line 6 - **demesne** - estate . . . Line 7 - **serene** - atmosphere . . . Line 10 - **ken** - range of sight . . . Line 11- **Cortez** - Vasco Nunez de Balboa, not Hernando Cortez, was the first European to sight the Pacific from Darien, a peak in Panama.

_45. The tone also changes from the octave's respectful but dispassionate assessment of reading to the sestet's (A) Adulation and reverence for God's many wonders (B) Smugness and self-satisfaction with human accomplishments (C) Repugnance and disgust with the evil mortals enjoy (D) Arrogance and contempt for Cortez's lack of accomplishments (E) Excitement and awe at the wonders discovered through reading.

_46. The following similes are used in the concluding sestet to convey the speaker's changed attitude:
    I. He compares his enthusiasm to that of someone who has perhaps seen a new planet through a telescope.

II. He compares his elation to that of an explorer who has seen an eagle in its wild habitat.

III. He compares his astonishment to that of Cortez's completely surprising discovery of a new ocean on the other side of the mountain.

(A) I only (B) II only (C) III only (D) I & II only (E) I, II & III

_47. A calm and measured movement can be seen in the octave, but the sestet's movement conveys the speaker's heightened emotions. Keats reinforces this flurry of feelings by manipulating the syntax so that the predominate iambic pentameter is accompanied with (A) Dashes and run-on lines (B) Balanced sentences (C) Periodic thoughts (D) Compound-complex sentence structure (E) Loose sentence construction.

_48. When the speaker refers to Hernando Cortez as a means of creating a visual representation of the emotional intensity experienced by the speaker, he is making use of which stylistic device? (A) Personification (B) Metonymy (C) Oxymoron (D) Allusion (E) Metaphor.

_49. All BUT one of the following words are chosen by John Keats in the sestet to represents intensity: (A) "Swims" (B) "Eagle eyes" (C) "Silent" (D) "Wild surmise" (E) "Deepbrowed."

_50. The sonnet ends leaving both the speaker and the explorer (A) Stranded on a peak (B) Lost in the Pacific Ocean (C) Looking at each other (D) Contemplating further discoveries (E) Staring at the Pacific.

Practice Test 3:
"Use A PEN"

ENGLISH
LITERATURE AND COMPOSITION
SECTION II
Time - 2 hours
Number of questions - 3
Percent of total grade - 55

Each question counts as one-third of the total essay score.
Question 1 Essay -- Suggested time. . . . . 40 minutes
Question 2 Essay -- Suggested time. . . . . 40 minutes
Question 3 Essay -- Suggested time. . . . . 40 minutes

Section II of this examination requires answers in essay form. To help you use your time well, the coordinator will announce the time at which each question should be completed. If you finished any question before the time is announced, you may go on to the following question. If you finish the examination in less than the time allotted, you may go back and work on any essay you want.

The quality of the composition will be considered in the scoring of all essay questions. Essays will be judged on their clarity and effectiveness in dealing with the topics. In response to Question 3, select only a work of literary merit that will be appropriate to the question. A general rule of thumb is to use works of the same quality as those you have been reading during your Advanced Placements year(s).

After completing each question, you should check your essay for accuracy and punctuation, spelling, and diction; you Are advised, however, not to attempt many long corrections. Remember that quality is far more important than quantity.

You should write your essays with a pen, preferably in black or dark blue ink. If you must use a pencil, be sure it has a well-sharpened point. Be sure to write CLEARLY and LEGIBLY. Cross out any errors you make.

The questions for Section II are printed in the green insert. Use the green insert to organize your answers and for scratch work, but write your answers in the pink essay booklet. Answer questions in order and number each answer as the question is numbered in the examination. Do not skip lines. Begin each answer on a new page in the pink essay booklet.

Note: These directions are copied from the essay section of *The 1994 AP English Literature and Composition: Free-Response Scoring Guide with Multiple-Choice Section* © Copyright 1995 by College Entrance Examination Board and Educational Testing Service. All rights reserved.

ENGLISH LITERATURE AND COMPOSITION
SECTION II

Total Time -- 2 hours

Question 1

(Suggested time — 40 minutes. This question counts one-third of the total)

Read the following excerpt from *Narrative of the Life of Frederick Douglass, An American Slave*. Then write a careful analysis of how the narrator reveals the character of Mr. Austin Gore. You may emphasize whichever literary techniques (e. g. tone, selection of detail, syntax - such as parallelism or balanced sentence structure - point of view, irony, imagery, diction, anecdote, choice of tense, and so forth) you find most significant.

Mr. Hopkins remained but a short time in the office of overseer. Why his career was so short, I do not know, but suppose he lacked the necessary severity to suit Colonel Lloyd. Mr. Hopkins was succeeded by Mr. Austin Gore, a man possessing, in an eminent degree, all those traits of character indispensable to what is called a first-rate overseer. Mr. Gore had served Colonel Lloyd, in the capacity of overseer, upon one of the out-farms, and had shown himself worthy of the high station of overseer upon the home or Great House Farm.

Mr. Gore was proud, ambitious, and persevering. He was artful, cruel, and obdurate. He was just the man for such a place, and it was just the place for such a man. It afforded scope for the full exercise of all his powers, and he seemed to be perfectly at home in it. He was one of those who could torture the slightest look, word, or gesture, on the part of the slave, into impudence, and would treat it accordingly. There must be no answering back to him; no explanation was allowed a slave, showing himself to have been wrongfully accused. Mr. Gore acted fully up to the maximum laid down by slaveholders -- "It is better that a dozen slaves suffer under the lash, than that the overseer should be convicted, in the presence of the slaves, of having been at fault." No matter how innocent a slave might be -- it availed him nothing, when accused by Mr. Gore of any misdemeanor. To be accused was to be convicted, and to be convicted was to be punished; the one always followed the other with immutable certainty. To escape punishment was to escape accusation; and few slaves had the fortune to do either, under the overseership of Mr. Gore. He was just proud enough to demand the most debasing homage of the slave, and quite servile enough to crouch, himself, at the feet of the master. He was ambitious enough to be contented with nothing short of the highest rank of overseers, and persevering enough to reach the height of his ambition. He was cruel enough to inflict the severest punishment, artful enough to descend to the lowest trickery, and obdurate enough to be insensible to the voice of a reproving conscience. He was, of all the overseers, the most dreaded by the slaves. His presence was painful; his eye flashed confusion; and seldom was his sharp, shrill voice heard, without producing horror and trembling in their ranks.

Mr. Gore was a grave man, and, though a young man, he indulged in no jokes, said no funny words, seldom smiled. His words were in perfect keeping with his looks, and his looks were in perfect keeping with his words. Overseer will sometimes indulge in a witty word, even with the slaves; not so with Mr. Gore. He spoke but to command, and commanded but to be obeyed; he dealt sparingly with his words, and bountifully with his whip, never using the former where the latter would answer as well. When he whipped, he seemed to do so from a sense of duty, and feared no consequences. He did nothing reluctantly, no matter how disagreeable; always at his post, never inconsistent. He never promised but to fulfill. He was, in a word, a man of the most inflexible firmness and stone-like coolness.

His savage barbarity was equalled only by the consummate coolness with which he committed the grossest and most savage deeds upon the slaves under his charge. Mr. Gore once undertook to whip one of Colonel Lloyd's slaves, by the name of Demby. He had given Demby but few stripes, when, to get rid of the scourging, he ran and plunged himself into the creek, and stood there at the depth of his shoulders, refusing to come out. Mr. Gore told him that he would give him three calls, and that, if he did not come out after the third call, he would shoot him. The first call was given. Demby made no response, but stood his ground. The second and third calls were given with the same result. Mr. Gore, then, without consultation or deliberation with anyone, not even giving Demby an additional call, raised his musket to his face, taking deadly aim at his standing victim, and in an instant poor Demby was no more. His mangled body sank out of sight, and blood and brains marked the spot where he had stood.

A thrill of horror flashed through every soul upon the plantation, excepting Mr. Gore. He alone seemed cool and collected. He was asked by Colonel Lloyd and my old master, why he resorted to this extraordinary expedient. His reply was (as well as I could remember), that Demby had become unmanageable. He was setting a dangerous example to the other slaves, -- one which, if suffered to pass without some such demonstration on his part, would finally lead to the total subversion of all law and order on the plantation. He argued that if one slave refused to be corrected, and escaped with his life, the other slaves would soon copy his example; the result of which would be, the freedom of the slaves, and the enslavement of the whites. Mr. Gore's defence was satisfactory. He was continued in his station as overseer upon the home plantation. His fame as an overseer went abroad. His horrid crime was not even submitted to judicial investigation. It was committed in the presence of slaves, and they of course could neither institute a suit, nor testify against him; and thus the guilty perpetrator of one of the bloodiest and most foul murders goes unwhipped of justice, and uncensured by the community in which he lives. Mr. Gore lived in St. Michael's, Talbot county, Maryland, when I left there; and if he is still alive, he very probably lives there now; and if so, he is now, as he was then, as highly esteemed and as much respected as though his guilty soul had not been stained with his brother's blood.

Question 2
(Suggested time — 40 minutes. This question counts one-third of the total)

The following two poems are written about death and pride. Read the poems carefully. Then write a carefully reasoned essay in which you analyze how each poet manipulates the language to convey a somewhat similar view.

Death Be Not Proud

> Death be not proud, though some have called thee
> Mighty and dreadful, for thou art not so,
> For those whom thou think'st thou dost overthrow
> Die not, poor death, nor yet canst thou kill me;
> From rest and sleep, which but thy pictures be,
> Much pleasure, then from thee, much more must flow,
> And soonest our best men with thee do go,
> Rest of their bones, and soul's delivery.
> Thou art slave to fate, chance, kings, and desperate
>   men,
> And dost with poison, war, and sickness dwell,
> And poppy, or charms, can make us sleep as well,
> And better than thy stroke; why swellest thou then?
> One short sleep past, we wake eternally,
> And death shall be no more, Death thou shalt die.
>   John Donne
>   (1572-1631)

Ozymandias

I met a traveler from an antique land,
Who said -- "Two vast and trunkless legs of stone
Stand in the desert . . . . Near them, on the sand,
Half sunk a shattered visage lies, whose frown,
And wrinkled lip, and sneer of cold command,
Tell that its sculptor well those passions read
Which yet survive, stamped on these lifeless things,
The hand that mocked them, and the heart that fed;
And on the pedestal, these words appear:
My name is Ozymandias, King of Kings,
Look on my works, ye mighty, and despair!
Nothing beside remains. Round the decay
Of that colossal wreck, boundless and bare
The lone and level sands stretch far away.

Percy Bysshe Shelly
(1792-1822)

Question 3

(Suggested time - 40 minutes. This questions counts
one-third of the total essay score.)

Anton Chekhov indicated in a letter to A. S. Souvorin,
October 27, 1888, that a writer should never confuse "solving
a problem" with "stating a problem. It is only the second that
is obligatory for the artist." It is the artists' duty to present the
right questions; the answers must be given by the reader in
their own light.

In an essay, discuss the ending of a work of literary
merit. With Chekhov's philosophy in mind, discuss how significant closure requires that the reader adide by or adjust to
ambiguity or uncertainty. Explain how or why the ending
appropriately or inappropriately concludes the work. Do not
merely summarize the plot.

Choose a novel or play by one of the following authors or another author of comparable merit.

Jane Austen	Carson McCullers
Joseph Conrad	Arthur Miller
George Eliot	Herman Melville
Louise Erdich	Toni Morrison
William Faulkner	Vladimir Nabokov
Henry Fielding	Sean O'Casey
Lorraine Hansberry	Eugene O'Neill
Thomas Hardy	Cynthia Ozick
Lillian Hellman	Harold Pinter
Zora Neal Hurston	Jean Rhys
Henry James	William Shakespeare
James Joyce	George Bernard Shaw
D. H. Lawrence	Jonathan Swift
Katherine Mansfield	Alice Walker
Eudora Welty	Edith Wharton

PRACTICE TEST 3 SCORING

NOTE: See separate teacher's guide addendum for answers and explanations for all multiple-choice tests in this book. Add the results of your scores below to determine your AP Grade:

Section I: Multiple-Choice (Total)

_____ - (.25 X _____) = _____ X 1.35 =_____

Number Correct	Number Wrong	Multiple-Choice Score	Weighted Score Section I

Section II: Free-Response

Writing: Essay 1: _____ X   3.0556 = _____

Do not round

Writing: Essay 2: _____ X   3.0556 = _____

Do not round

Writing: Essay 3: _____ X   3.0556 = _____

Do not round

Use CHECKLISTS or RUBRICS on the preceding pages to grade your essays.

Weighted Section II Score

Do not round

Composite Score:

_____ + _____ = _____

Weighted Multiple-Choice Score	Weighted Free-Response Score	**Composite**

Composite Score	AP Grade
150 - 107 (71%)	5
106 - 93 (62%)	4
92 - 74 (49%)	3
73 - 44 (29%)	2
43 - 0	1

Answers and Explanations

To Practice Test 3:
Section II: Essay

Checklist for

Question 1

from *Narrative of the Life of Frederick Douglass, An American Slave* by Frederick Douglass

STEP 1: Subtract one point for each item **not checked** from the checklist below:

___-___1. The writer demonstrates a perceptive understanding of Mr. Austin Gore's character.

___-___2. The writer analyzes how the author uses literary techniques (e. g. tone, selection of detail, syntax - such as parallelism or balanced sentence structure - point of view, irony, imagery, diction, anecdote, choice of tense, and so forth) to characterize Mr. Gore.

___-___3. The writer demonstrates a perceptive understanding of how the language is manipulated by Frederick Douglass to reveal Mr. Gore's character.

___-___4. The writer makes apt (a minimum of three embedded bits of quotes per paragraph) and specific (detailed and appropriate) reference to the texts.

___-___5. The writer offers a convincing interpretation of the power of the character sketch.

___-___6. The writer demonstrates an ability to read perceptively by saying something beyond the easy and obvious to grasp

___-___7. The writer demonstrates a control over the virtues of effective communication, including the language unique to literary criticism.

___-___8. The writer's organization is implicit and original, yet communicates a clear message.

___-___9. The writer's diction, sentence structure, and grammar aid in communicating a clear message.

MAXIMUM SCORE RESULTS: Grader 1 _____

MAXIMUM SCORE RESULTS: Grader 2 _____

STEP 2: Subtract one point from the results of step 1 for each item **checked** from the rubrics list below. NOTE: To avoid a negative number, you may not have any more checks here than the total on the left.

___-___1. The writer's definition of Mr. Gore's personality is oversimplified or vague.

___-___2. The writer discusses the use of tone, selection of detail, syntax - such as parallelism or balanced sentence structure - point of view, irony, imagery, diction, anecdote, choice of tense, and so forth with limited purpose or with inappropriate examples.

___-___3. The connection between language and characterization is less clear than those of the top-scoring essays.

___-___4. The writer's use of quotes is awkward, inappropriate, or uninteresting.

___-___5. The writer's interpretation does not address the powerful effect of Mr. Gore's character .

___-___6. The writer displays simplistic thinking.

___-___7. The writer misuses the literary term(s) addressed in the question or omits them partially or entirely.

___-___8. The organization of this essay is less original or implicit than those of the top-scoring essays.

___-___9. The essay reveals consistent weakness in grammar and/or other basic elements of composition.

RESULTS:

Grader 1: _____ - _____ = _____
                Step 1 Score   Step 2 Score

Grader 2: _____ - _____ = _____
                Step 1 Score   Step 2 Score

Grader 1 Score + Grader 2 Score = _____

Above sum /
divided by 2 =

Score for essay

Answers and Explanations

To Practice Test 3:
Section II: AP Rubrics

Rubrics for Question 1

from *Narrative of the Life of Frederick Douglass, An American Slave* by Frederick Douglass

8-9   With apt and specific references to the story, these well-organized and well-written essays clearly analyze how Frederick Douglass uses literary techniques (e. g. tone, selection of detail, syntax - such as parallelism or balanced sentence structure - point of view, irony, imagery, diction, anecdote, choice of tense, and so forth) to characterize Mr. Gore. The best of these essays will acknowledge and then address the complexity of the characterization. While not without flaws, these papers will demonstrate an understanding of the text as well as consistent control over the elements of effective composition. These writers read with perception and express their ideas with clarity and skill.

6-7   These papers also analyze how Frederick Douglass uses literary techniques to characterize Mr. Gore, but they are less incisive, developed or aptly supported than papers in the highest range. They deal accurately with technique as a means by which a writer brings a character to life, but they are less effective or less thorough in their analysis than are the 8-9 essays. These essays demonstrate the writer's ability to express ideas clearly, but they do so with less maturity and precision than the best papers.

5   These essays are superficial. They respond to the assignment without important errors in composition, but they miss the complexity of Douglass's use of literary techniques and offer a perfunctory analysis of how those techniques are used to characterize Mr. Gore. Often, the analysis is vague, mechanical, or inadequately supported. While the writing is sufficient to convey the writer's thoughts, these essays are not as well-conceived, organized, or developed as the upper half papers. Usually, they reveal simplistic thinking and/or immature writing.

3-4   These lower half essays reflect an incomplete understanding of the story and fail to respond adequately to the question. The discussion of how Douglass uses literary techniques to characterize Mr. Gore may be inaccurate or unclear, misguided or underdeveloped; these papers may paraphrase rather than analyze. The analysis of technique will likely be meager and unconvincing. Generally, the writing demonstrates weak control of such elements as diction, organization, syntax, or grammar. These essays typically contain recurrent stylistic flaws and/or misreadings and lack persuasive evidence from the text.

1-2   These essays compound the weaknesses of the essays in the 3-4 range. They seriously misunderstand the character or fail to respond to the question. Frequently, they are unacceptably brief. Often poorly written of several counts, they may contain many distracting errors in grammar and mechanics. Although some attempt may have been made to answer the question, the writer's views typically are presented with little clarity, organization, coherence, or supporting evidence. Essays that are especially inexact, vacuous, and/or mechanically unsound should be scored 1.

0   This is a response with no more than a reference to the task.

-        Indicates a blank response, or one that is completely off-topic.

Answers and Explanations

To Practice Test 3:
Section II: Results
of Essay 1

from *Narrative of the Life of Frederick Douglass, An American Slave*
by Frederick Douglass

1-3. The writer demonstrates a perceptive understanding of
Mr. Austin Gore's character, analyzing how the author uses
literary techniques (e. g. tone, selection of detail, syntax - such
as parallelism or balanced sentence structure - point of view,
irony, imagery, diction, anecdote, choice of tense, and so forth)
to characterize Mr. Gore.

> A. Douglass's initial choice of positive diction ironi-
> cally are used in a negative sense as the character
> sketch is developed.
> B. Douglas uses an ambiguous point-counter point
> organization showing how Mr. Gore is respectful and
> civil in his white world, yet harsh and cruel as an over-
> seer.
> C. The passage is littered with condemning anecdotes
> that contrast with the positive generalizations of Gore.
> D. Rearranging words and varying sentence struc-
> ture allows Mr. Douglass to draw readers in, letting
> them experience his drastically changing impressions
> of the overseer, Mr. Austin Gore.

4-5. The writer makes apt (a minimum of three embedded
bits of quotes per paragraph) and specific (detailed and appropriate) reference to the text, offering a convincing interpretation of Douglass's sketch.

> A. Gore held the ambition to become the best over-
> seer -- "persevering" to "reach the height of his ambi-
> tion."
> B. Mr. Gore's voice was seldom heard "without pro-
> ducing horror and trembling in their ranks."
> C. Ironically, Mr. Gore remained highly esteemed, as
> if "his guilty soul had not been stained with his
> brother's blood."

6. The writer demonstrates an ability to read perceptively by saying something beyond the easy and obvious to grasp.

A. Douglass paints an initially objective picture of Mr. Gore as a character striving for achievement in a harsh and cruel environment.

B. In essence, Douglass's portrait of Mr. Gore is a 3D picture, respecting him for his "sense of duty," pitying him for his "inflexible firmness," and hating him for his "savage barbarity."

8. Do not force the same organization into every essay. Avoid topic sentences that name the device and make a connection to the view, yet say nothing specific or misread Douglass's revelation of Gore's character..

A. Douglass's use of positive words conveyed that he thought highly of Mr. Gore. (This misread Douglass's view.)

B. Douglass uses syntax to reveal Mr. Gore's character.

C. Douglass uses parallelism and balanced sentence structure to reveal Mr. Gore's demeanor.

Rather, the writer's organization should be implicit and original, yet communicating a clear message. The highest scores will discuss the language of the passage in a natural way, attaching an individual interpretation to the writing .

A. Although Douglass appears to respect Gore at first, it becomes increasingly clear that his attitude is quite the opposite.

B. Mr. Austin Gore, a first-rate overseer, worthy of a high station like that of the overseer of the Great House Farm, lacked a guiltless soul.

7, 9. The writer demonstrates a control over the virtues of effective communication, including the language unique to literary criticism, the writer's diction, sentence structure, and grammar. Correct the following:

A. There are many descriptive adjectives of Gore's personality both with positive and negative connotations.

B. Depending upon many different factors, such as race, religion and background experience, everyone has unique perceptions of someone's personality.

C. In Douglass's excerpt, an American slave, Douglass's life story is relayed, where he lived, and the place he encountered.

Answers and Explanations

To Practice Test 3:
Section II: Essay

Checklist for Question 2
from John Donne's "Death Be Not Proud" and
Percy Bysshe Shelly's "Ozmandias"

STEP 1: Subtract one point for each item **not checked** from the checklist below:

___-___1. The definition of the speakers' views of pride and death demonstrate a perceptive understanding of each of the works.

___-___2. The essay analyzes how such rhetorical or stylistic devices as figurative language, imagery, and irony are used differently by each author to convey a somewhat similar view.

___-___3. The essay continually shows the connection between the speakers' attitudes and the language devices used to convey that attitude.

___-___4. The essay supports the discussion of each language device with apt (a minimum of three embedded bits of quotes per paragraph) and specific (detailed and appropriate) reference to the both poems.

___-___5. Though not without flaws, these papers offer a convincing interpretation of both poems.

___-___6. The essay demonstrates the writer's ability to read perceptively .

___-___7. The writer demonstrates a control over the virtues of effective communication, including the language unique to literary criticism.

___-___8. The writer's organization is implicit and original, yet communicates a clear message.

___-___9. The writer's diction, sentence structure, and grammar aid in communicating a clear message.

MAXIMUM SCORE RESULTS: Grader 1 _____

MAXIMUM SCORE RESULTS: Grader 2 _____

STEP 2: Subtract one point from the results of step 1 for each item **checked** from the rubrics list below. NOTE: To avoid a negative number, you may not have any more checks here than the total on the left.

___-___1. The writer fails to respond adequately to part(s) of the question by simply defining the attitude, or simply naming the language devices used, or both.

___-___2. The writer's discussion of how such devices as figurative language, imagery, and irony are used differently by each author to convey a somewhat similar view may be vague, mechanical, or inadequately supported.

___-___3. The connection between the evidence and the authors' probable or intended attitudes becomes lost in part of the discussion.

___-___4. Although adequate in number, the evidence in this essay is not as convincing as that of the top scoring essays. In addition, their analysis is likely to be briefer and less persuasive.

___-___5. The writer simply paraphrases each poem or has minor flaws in interpretation.

___-___6. The writer deals with the assigned task without major flaws, but has little to say beyond what is easy and obvious to grasp.

___-___7. The writer demonstrates uncertain control over the qualities of college-level composition.

___-___8. While the writing is sufficient to convey the writer's thoughts, these essays are not as well-conceived, organized, or developed as the upper half papers.

___-___9. The essay reveals consistent weakness in grammar and/or other basic elements of composition. Often they reveal simplistic thinking and/or immature writing.

RESULTS:

Grader 1: _____ - _____ = _____
          Step 1 Score   Step 2 Score

Grader 2: _____ - _____ = _____
          Step 1 Score   Step 2 Score

Grader 1 Score + Grader 2 Score = _____

Above sum /
divided by 2 =

Score for essay

Answers and Explanations

To Practice Test 3:
Section II: AP Rubrics

Rubrics for Question 2

from John Donne's "Death Be Not Proud" and
Percy Bysshe Shelly's "Ozymandias"

8-9   These well-written essays clearly demonstrate
an understanding of how each author manipulates the language to convey a somewhat similar view of pride and death.
With apt and specific reference, they analyze how such elements as figurative language, imagery, and irony are used differently by each poet to convey a somewhat similar view.
Though not without flaws, these papers offer convincing interpretations of both poems; they demonstrate the writer's
ability to read perceptively and write with clarity and skill.

6-7   These essays also demonstrate an understanding of the somewhat similar view of pride and death, but compared to the best essays, they are less thorough or less precise
in analyzing the differences between the use of such devices
as figurative language, imagery, and irony. In addition to minor flaws in interpretation, their analysis is likely to be briefer,
less well-supported and less incisive. These essays demonstrate the writer's ability to express ideas clearly, but with less
mastery and control than do papers in the 8-9 range.

5   These essay are superficial. The treatment of
the devices and the attitude is typically pedestrian. They deal
with the assigned task without major errors, but have little to
say beyond what is easy and obvious to grasp. Their understanding of how such devices as figurative language, imagery,
and irony contribute to the views may be vague, mechanical
or inadequately supported. While the writing is sufficient to
convey the writer's thoughts, these essays are not as well conceived, organized or developed as the upper half papers. Often they reveal simplistic thinking and/or immature writing.

5   These essays are superficial. The treatment of the devices and the attitude is typically pedestrian. They deal with the assigned task without major errors, but have little to say beyond the easy and obvious to grasp. Their understanding of how such devices as figurative language, imagery, and irony contribute differently to similar views may be vague, mechanical, or inadequately supported. While the writing is sufficient to convey the writer's thoughts, the essays are not as well-conceived, organized, or developed as the upper half papers. Often they reveal simplistic thinking and/or immature writing.

3-4   These lower half essays fail to respond adequately to part(s) of the question. They reflect an incomplete understanding of the somewhat similar view of pride and death seen in each poem, and/or their treatment of such language devices such as figurative language, imagery, and irony may be meager or unclear, inaccurate or irrelevant. The writing usually demonstrates uncertain control over the qualities of college-level composition. They usually contain recurrent stylistic flaws and/or misreadings and lack persuasive evidence from the text. These essays may paraphrase rather than analyze. Essays scored 3 exhibit more than one of the problems exhibited above; they are marred by significant misinterpretations, insufficient development, or serious omissions.

1-2   These essays compound the weaknesses of the essays in the 3-4 range. They seriously misread one or both of the poems. Frequently, they are unacceptably brief. Often poorly written of several counts, they may contain many distracting errors in grammar and mechanics. Although some attempt may have been made to answer the question, the writer's views typically are presented with little clarity, organization, coherence, or supporting evidence. Essays that are especially inexact, vacuous, and/or mechanically unsound should be scored 1.

0   This is a response with no more than a reference to the task.

-       Indicates a blank response, or one that is completely off-topic.

Answers and Explanations

To Practice Test 3:
Section II: Results
of Essay 2

from John Donne's "Death Be Not Proud" and
Percy Bysshe Shelly's "Ozymandias"

1-3. The definition of the speakers' views of pride and death
demonstrate a perceptive understanding of each of the works,
showing how such rhetorical or stylistic devices as figurative
language, imagery, and irony are used differently by each author to convey a somewhat similar view.

> B. Although both poets view pride as a sinful trait,
> Donne addresses death directly, chastising it for hav-
> ing pride.
> A. Shelly, on the other hand, uses a story of the dead
> Pharaoh, Ozmandias, whose monuments of pride have
> been destroyed by the sands of time, to portray this
> more subtly.
> C. In both cases, death is viewed, respectively, as
> unimportant or as a means of showing unimportance.

4-5. The essay supports the discussion of each language device with apt (a minimum of three embedded bits of quotes
per paragraph) and specific (detailed and appropriate) reference to the both poems, offer a convincing interpretation of
both poems.

> A. Donne remarks that some have called death
> "mighty and dreadful," making people a "slave to fate."
> B. All that if left of Ozmandias's once great empire is
> "lone and level sand."

8. Do not force the same organization into every essay. Avoid topic sentences that name the device and make a connection to the view, yet say nothing specific.

    A. Imagery is used to convey a similar view of death.

    B. Irony is used to covey a similar view of death.

    C. Figurative language is used to covey a similar view of death.

    D. Diction is an important element used by each poet to convey meaning.

Rather, the writer's organization should be implicit and original, yet communicating a clear message. The highest scores will discuss the language of the passage in a natural way, attaching an individual interpretation to the writing .

    A. Both poets indicate that death implies a certain loneliness for those whose pride is too excessive. (Note how this topic sentence addresses meaning. The rest of the paragraph would show how the poet manipulates the language to convey loneliness.)

    B. Both poets make ironic, almost satirical comments about death. (Note how this topic sentence addresses meaning. The rest of the paragraph would show how the poet manipulates the language to convey satire.)

7, 9. The writer demonstrates a control over the virtues of effective communication, including the language unique to literary criticism, the writer's diction, sentence structure, and grammar. Correct the following:

    A. There are millions of ways to express many types of feelings about death.

    B. In the poem by John Donne, he is expressing why death should not be proud.

    C. Death is looked upon in different ways by different people all around the world as a beginning of a new life or an ending to a perfect life.

    D. Both Donne and Shelly think that death is not a big deal like others make it out to be, only they use different techniques to express this thought.

    E. Both of the authors which wrote "Death Be Not Proud" and Ozmandias" view death a pride similarly.

Answers and Explanations

To Practice Test 3:
Section II: Essay

Checklist for Question 3

Open Question on AMBIGUITY OR UNCERTAINTY

STEP 1: Subtract one point for each item **not checked** from the checklist below:

___-___1. The writer selects a suitable novel or play in which significant closure requires that the reader abide by or adjust to ambiguity or uncertainty.

___-___2. The writer presents a reasonable explanation of the meaning of the work.

___-___3. The writer effectively explains how or why the ending appropriately <u>or</u> inappropriately concludes the work.

___-___4. The writer convincingly explains the ending's significance to the work as a whole.

___-___5. The writer makes apt and specific reference to the text.

___-___6. The writer avoids plot summary not relevant to the explanation of the role that the ending plays in the evocation of multiple meanings in the work.

___-___7. The writer discusses the literary work with sophistication, insight, and understanding.

___-___8. The writer's displays consistent control over the language unique to literary discussion.

___-___9. The writer's diction, sentence structure, organization, and grammar aid in communicating a clear message.

MAXIMUM SCORE RESULTS: Grader 1 _____

MAXIMUM SCORE RESULTS: Grader 2 _____

STEP 2: Subtract one point from the results of step 1 for each item **checked** from the rubrics list below. NOTE: To avoid a negative number, you may not have any more checks here than the total on the left.

___-___1. The writer's selection of a play or novel is not as appropriate as those of the higher scoring essays.

___-___2. The writer's explanation of the meaning of the work is less thorough, less specific, or less perceptive than those of the higher scoring essays.

___-___3. The writer's explanation of the appropriateness or inappropriateness of the selected work's ending may be vague, underdeveloped, or misguided.

___-___4. The writer's explanation of the ending's significance may be less convincing, mechanical, or inadequately related to the work as a whole.

___-___5. The writer's reference to the text lack the specificity of the higher scoring essays.

___-___6. The writer simply paraphrases the meaning of the work with little reference to how the ending's ambiguity or uncertainty elicits multiple meanings in the work.

___-___7. The writer says nothing beyond the easy and obvious to grasp.

___-___8. The writer misuses the literary term(s) necessary to literary discussion or omits them partially or entirely.

___-___9. The essay contains distracting errors in grammar and mechanics.

RESULTS:

Grader 1: _____ - _____ = _____
       Step 1 Score   Step 2 Score

Grader 2: _____ - _____ = _____
       Step 1 Score   Step 2 Score

Grader 1 Score + Grader 2 Score = _____

Above sum /
divided by 2 =

Score for essay

Answers and Explanations

To Practice Test 3:
Section II: AP Rubrics

Rubrics for Question 3

Open Question on AMBIGUITY OR UNCERTAINTY

8-9   These well-written essays identify the "ambiguity or uncertainty" evident in the ending of a novel or play of literary merit, and they explain convincingly its significance to the work as a whole. These essays will be specific in their references to the text, cogent in their explications, and free of plot summary not related to how significant closure requires that the reader abide by or adjust to ambiguity or uncertainty. These essays need not be without error, but they exhibit the writer's ability to discuss a literary work with insight and understanding, as well as the writer's ability to control an appropriate range of the elements of effective composition.

6-7   These essays also identify the "ambiguity or uncertainty" evident in the ending of a novel or play of literary merit. In addition, they explain the significance of that ending to the work as a whole. Their analysis, however, is less thorough, less perceptive, or less specific than of 8-9 papers. Though not as convincing in their discussion, these essays are generally well-written. They demonstrate the writer's ability to explain how an ending of the kind Chekhov describes works relative to the novel or play as a whole, but they are less sophisticated in their analysis and less consistent in their command of the elements of effective college-level expository prose than are essays scored 8-9.

5   Superficiality characterizes these essays. They may choose an appropriate ending, but their explanation of how significant closure requires that the reader abide by or adjust to ambiguity or uncertainty is vague or oversimplified. Their discussion of meaning may also be pedestrian or mechanical. Typically, these essays reveal unsophisticated thinking and/or immature writing. They usually demonstrate inconsistent control over the elements of effective composition and are not as well-conceived, organized, or developed as upper-half papers. The writing, however, is adequate to convey the writer's views.

3-4   These lower half essays may not choose an ending that creates "ambiguity or uncertainty"; or they may have failed to explain the significance of that ending to the work as a whole. Their analysis may be unpersuasive, perfunctory, underdeveloped, or misguided. Often, their discussion is inaccurate or not clearly related to the question. The writing may convey the writer's ideas, but it reveals weak control such elements as the language unique to literary discussion, diction, organization, syntax, or grammar. These essays may contain important misinterpretations of the novel or play, inadequate supporting evidence, and/or paraphrase and plot summary rather than analysis.

1-2   These essays compound the weaknesses of the papers in the 3-4 range. They seriously misread the play or novel, or seriously misinterpret the ending they have chosen. Frequently, they are unacceptably brief. Often poorly written on several counts, they may contain many distracting errors in grammar and mechanics. Although some attempt may have been made to answer the question, the writer's views typically are presented with little clarity, organization, coherence, or supporting evidence. Essay that are especially vacuous, ill-organized, illogically argued, and/or mechanically unsound should be scored 1.

0   This is a response with no more than a reference to the task.

-       Indicates a blank response, or one that is wholly unrelated to the assignment.

A Final Thought on the Power of Words
"PUNCH, BROTHERS, PUNCH" by Mark Twain

Will the reader please to cast his eye over the following lines, and see if he can discover anything harmful in them?

Conductor, when you receive a fare,
Punch in the presence of the passenjare!
A blue trip slip for an eight-cent fare,
A buff trip slip for a six-cent fare,
A pink trip slip for a three-cent fare,
CHORUS
Punch, brothers! punch with care!
Punch in the presence of the passenjare!

I came across these jingling rhymes in the newspaper, a little while ago, and read them a couple of times. They took instant and entire possession of me. All through breakfast they went waltzing through my brain; and when, at last, I rolled up the napkin, I could not tell whether I had eaten anything or not. I had carefully laid out my day's work the day before -- a thrilling tragedy in the novel which I am writing. I went to my den my deed of blood. I took up my pen, but all I could get it to say was "Punch in the presence of the passenjare!" I fought hard for an hour but it was useless. My head kept humming, "A blue trip slip for an eight-cent fare, A buff trip slip for a six-cent fare," and so on and so on, without peace or respite. The day's work was ruined -- I could see plainly enough. I gave up and drifted down-town, and presently discovered that my feet were keeping time to that relentless jingle. When I could stand it no longer I altered my step. But it did no good; those rhymes accommodated themselves to the new step and went on harassing me just as before. I returned home, and suffered all the afternoon; suffered all through an unconscious and unrefreshing dinner; suffered, and cried, and jingled all through the evening; went to bed and rolled, tossed, and jingled right along, the same as ever; got up at midnight frantic, and tried to read; but there was nothing visible upon the whirling page except, "Punch! punch in the presence of the passenjare." By sunrise I was out of my mind, and everybody marveled and was distressed at the idiotic burden of my ravings --"Punch! oh, punch! punch in the presence of the passenjare!"

Two days later on a Saturday morning, I arose, a tottering wreck, and went forth to fulfill an engagement with a valued friend. . . . Mr. ___ talked, talked, talked -- as is his wont. . . . At the end of a mile , Mr. ___ said:

"Mark, are you sick? I never in my life saw a man so haggard and worn and absent-minded. Say something, do!"

. . . . I began at the beginning and repeated all the lines.

My friend's face lighted with interest. He said:

"Why what a captivating jingle it is! It is almost music. It flows along so nicely. I have nearly caught the rhymes myself. Say them over just once more, and them I'll have them, sure."

I said them over. Then Mr. ___ said them. He made one little mistake, which I corrected. The next time and the next he got them right. Now a great burden seemed to tumble from my shoulders. That torturing jingle departed out of my brain, and a grateful sense of rest and peace descended upon me. I was light-hearted enough to sing; and I did sing for half an hour, straight along, as we went jogging homeward. Then my freed tongue found blessed speech again, and the pent talk of many a weary hour began to gush and flow. It flowed on and on, joyously, jubilantly, until the fountain was empty and dry. As I wrung my friend's hand at parting, I said:

"Haven't we had a royal good time! But now I remember, you haven't said a word for two hours. Come, come, out with something.

The Rev. Mr. ___ turned a lack-luster eye upon me, drew a deep sigh, and said, without animation, without apparent consciousness:

"Punch, brothers, punch with care! Punch in the presence of the passenjare!"

A pang shot through me as I said to myself, "Poor fellow, poor fellow! *he* has got it, now."

I did not see Mr. ___ for two or three days after that. Then, on Tuesday evening, he staggered into my presence and sat dejectedly into a seat. He was pale, worn; he was a wreck.

. . . . How did I finally save him from an asylum? I took him to a neighboring university and made him discharge the burden of his persecuting rhymes into the eager ears of the poor, unthinking students. How is it with *them*, now? The result is too sad to tell. Why did I write this article? It was for a worthy, even a noble purpose. It was to warn you, reader, if you should come across those merciless rhymes, to avoid them -- avoid them as you would the pestilence!

Plan Press Inc.

921 Pembina Trail• Detroit Lakes, MN 56501

ORDERING INFORMATION

Date _____-_____-_____   Purchase Order Number _____

SHIP TO: **BILL TO:**

_____   _____
Name of High School   Independent School District #

_____   _____
Contact Name   Contact Name or Department

_____   _____
Street Address / PO Box   Street Address / PO Box

_____   _____
City, State Zip   City, State Zip

ITEM # PRODUCT	PRICE PER COPY	QUANTITY	TOTAL
1001 *A Practical AP LANGUAGE Guide*	$18.95	_____	_____
1002 AP LANGUAGE ANS/EXPLANATIONS	$ 4.00	_____	_____
2001 *A Practical AP LITERATURE Guide*	$18.95	_____	_____
2002 AP LITERATURE ANS/EXPLANATIONS	$ 4.00	_____	_____

- -

SUBTOTAL   _____

Sales Tax (None if School)   _____

Shipping & Handling ($6.00 Minimum,
7-25 items = $1.00 per item, Larger Orders= Cost) _____

Please make check payable to:
Plan Press Inc, 921 Pembina Trail   TOTAL _____
Detroit Lakes, MN 56501